Coming home to You

A Handbook for Personal Transformation

**With powerful practical exercises
to put your best life into action**

Mary McGuire

Book cover design and formatting services by BookCoverCafe.com

www.findyourjoyfullife.com

ISBN:
978-1-9997041-0-0 (pbk)
978-1-9997041-1-7 (ebk)

This Book Is For You If You...

- are constantly questioning if you are good enough;
- feel your life is on a downward spiral, living to work and working to live;
- feel like you are always looking for the 'right' answer;
- have lost the joy and passion you once felt;
- feel like you are suppressing long held emotions, but are unsure how to release them;
- are constantly worried, stressed and anxious; or
- know you need to give yourself time and energy to change your life, but are unsure where to begin.

This Book Will Help You When You...

- know that even in the most difficult of circumstances, you have the ability to turn your life around;
- want to discover how to take control of and improve your: thoughts; feelings; health; and wellbeing, step by step; and
- are ready to recognise your need for happiness and willing to spend the time reclaiming it.

How to Use this Book

This book can be read fully from cover to cover if you wish and enjoyed for the ideas and concepts it shares.

However, if you are looking to make long and lasting change in your life, it is best to treat this book like a practical handbook. When we have a book that is designed to guide or help us with certain situations we tend to read and re-read it at the point of need. This way, the knowledge that is most pertinent can reach us exactly when we need it.

From Chapter Two, each chapter deals with a single subject. At the end of the chapters are practical exercises for you to try. Completing the exercises will help you receive the most benefit from this book and its teachings.

At the end of the book, there are references for further reading and where to go for further help, including the author's website: Findyourjoyfullife.com.

About the Author

Mary McGuire lives between England and Ireland with her partner. A long-time transformation consultant for global companies, her own life went through a dramatic turnaround after illness in 2008 took away much of what she took for granted  in her life, including her health. Through a process of trial and error, she started to wake up to her spirituality, the nature of happiness and develop a rich inner life. This freed her from the internal and harmful thought cycles that had led to much of her own unhappiness and allowed her to regain a full and vibrant state of health.

As her awareness of the power of thoughts grew, she became more mindful and life opened in wonderful ways. This, her first book, marks her journey from lost to found, and shares the many ways she has learnt to live a joyful life. She believes that this is possible for everyone to achieve and this is the motivation behind this book.

Mary holds a BA (Hons) in Social Work, An MBA in Business and an MSc in Organisational Development. After many years working with international companies on organisational transformation, her focus is moving to personal transformation, where she believes the biggest impact can be made in the world.

*For **Joy**, who has brought more than a lifetime's worth of Joy into my life. Thank you for the love, encouragement and support that made this book possible.*

Acknowledgements

Thanks go to Wendy Yorke, my literary coach and editor. Having her guiding me at every stage, brought out the story that needed to be told. Thanks to my proof reader and reviewer extraordinaire, Joy. If it didn't make the first cut, it didn't get printed.

There are many others who have helped me along my journey. To Mario Van Boeschoten, my one-time mentor I thank you for widening my horizons when I was ripe to learn. To Dame Stephanie Shirley, thank you for setting standards which seemed impossibly high at the time, but stood me in good stead in the long-term. To my parents, I am grateful for the resilience our circumstances brought forth. It has made me fearless and determined. Thank you also to my friends and family who have been a constant source of support and encouragement along the way. The final cut was decided by Anna Yorke, so thank you for such a thorough proof reading. And this book would not have been half so beautiful without Anthony and his great team at BookCoverCafe.com. I knew I was in safe hands.

Coming Home to You

A Handbook for Personal Transformation

"Taking the journey home to you, one step at a time will reap the most amazing rewards. Be free, be brave and enjoy every minute of this wonderful life you have."

Let the transformation begin

With powerful practical exercises to put your best life into action

By Mary McGuire

Illustrations by Ecaterina Leascenco

Need another way to digest this book?

Haven't got time to read the full version?

Prefer to listen to it on the run?
Visit: **http://findyourjoyfullife.com/book-launch**

Just click the link and you will get access to:

- An audio of Chapter 13 – Freeing your spiritual self.
- A special discount code to access the full audio book
- Three free worksheets from the book to support your transformation.
- You will also be on a first to know basis for future launches and special discounts.

Contents

Introduction

The motivation behind this book is to share my journey with you. To show you that no matter how difficult your beginnings and how many obstacles you face, it is possible to break free of a life of struggle, stress and ill health. Even if it does not seem possible right now, this book will show you there is a way to turn your life into one of vibrant joy and harmony. That is quite a huge claim, which I do not make lightly. However, each of us has this inbuilt source of joy and happiness inside us. It is there from the moment we are born, to the moment we die. Even though for so much of our lives we are told the opposite; that we are no good, unlovable, worthless and unimportant. There is a truth, which sits behind these messages, that we are loved and lovable beyond measure. Reaching that deeper truth is the purpose of this book, to help you reconnect with that nurturing soul inside of you, which will show you the way out of your pain and into your light.

Most of what we are told or led to believe is far removed from this truth. Modern society has colluded to keep us in the dark, through its culture, structures and belief systems, which ultimately disempower us. The consequence is to remove us from our sense of self. We become a stranger to ourselves and enslaved by thoughts, emotions and beliefs, which keep us hidden from our true nature.

The good news is that by waking up to this realization and forming simple habits, we can lift ourselves out of this enslavement and find a path of true empowerment. This is the way to true healing and living the fullest, happiest life we can imagine.

To do this we have to be truly alive. We have to be willing to take a different path, one which will allow us to truly touch our inner nature and cast-off the roles and expectations placed on us by family, friends and society at large. This is everyone's natural birth right and this is why I want to share my story with you.

Let me tell you a little bit about myself and why I believe this call to action is required right now. Why a mass shift in our consciousness is needed to stop the world we live in from imploding, due to the mindless and un-awakened actions of the majority of people.

My day job for the last 20 years has been as an international change agent, working with global organisations usually at a point of, or in the midst of a crisis, requiring external intervention to help them turn their fortunes around. My work has brought me to many countries, many cultures and many worldviews.

My early career was in a very different sphere, though it also involved working in crisis situations with people needing help to make change. I worked as a social worker, in a poor inner city area, in North England, where impoverished and dysfunctional families lurched from one crisis to the next. They were the victims of circumstance, history and unhealthy patterns, which they found difficult to break.

By working across such a broad spectrum of humanity in a range of different environments, I have developed a unique perspective. I have seen both the powerful and the powerless, at points of anxiety and frustration, who felt unable to break the chains of despair of their current circumstances. Indeed, for many people I have encountered, they were unable to make the link between their actions and their situation.

They believed the two were randomly generated events on which they had no influence.

In addition to my observations, I have been on my own transformational journey, learning to move from a state of unawareness to awakened consciousness. This journey turned my reality upside down as the scales were removed from my eyes. I started to consider the world, not as a set of random circumstances in which I haplessly made my way through, but rather as a wondrous web of interconnectedness that is experienced and navigated through self-awareness. My experiences have convinced me of the need to wake up to a life, which abounds all around us, so we can start living the most joyous and enlightening life imaginable. But to do this we must debunk some of myths that get in the way of experiencing the magnificence of the world around us. This book will help you do that for yourself, by opening you up to new concepts and ideas and showing you through practical exercises how you can make the changes you want to see in your own life.

Chapter 1

My Story

The early years

Bullying was a feature of my life from a very young age and became a theme right up until my adulthood. I seemed destined to be the eternal victim, portrayed as the one less worthy, less confident, less deserving than her peers. There were many reasons for this, but perhaps the main reasons were that I lived in a rough inner-city neighbourhood, I was the youngest daughter of poorly-skilled parents and I had little by way of confidence or support around me to protect me from life's knocks. At every turn, I was told I wasn't good enough, I didn't fit in and I looked messy, dirty or worthless, in the eyes of other people.

Coming Home to You

I don't believe my situation was unique, for there are millions of children in the world trying to survive a difficult childhood, much like mine or worse. I was the daughter of Irish Catholic parents who struggled to make ends meet and who could hardly stand to be in each other's company. We were barely surviving from day to day and there was little in the way of nurturing or love available to us children. The constant threat of something running out – be it food, shelter, clothing or heat – was the same for probably every family down our street. But some families had a natural inbuilt resistance, which was lacking in our own.

While my mother worried about how to put food on the table and a roof over our heads, my father's concerns were much simpler; merely to know there was enough money for his next drink. This drove my mother out to many part-time jobs to try to make ends meet and my father to the local pub, to avoid worrying about such matters.

With both parents absent, we were left to roam around the streets of Birmingham, to do what we pleased. Although I had older siblings, the lack of cohesion inside the home meant we had little cohesion outside the home, leaving us to become lone wolfs, following our own path.

Given this backdrop, it's perhaps not surprising I occasionally became the victim of local bullies and street thugs. From an early age, I was introduced to the world of cruelty, violence and malice. But perhaps the greater sadness is the children who were as young as five or six, who became my torturers, had already learnt and were motivated to degrade and humiliate another human being to mask their own feelings of worthlessness.

The emotional wounds we develop at this tender age are perhaps the ones we bury the deepest and the one's which take the longest to surface in our journey to awakening and healing. We often use denial or simply brush over our traumatic experiences, deeming them perfectly normal, as our way of coping. But this denigrates our need for healing and denies our path to forgiveness.

At some point these negative and abusive experiences started to bury a belief deep in my psyche that I was not as good as other people. I would never be: good enough; clean enough; clever enough; and ultimately, I would never be lovable enough; to be worthy of other people's respect and love.

This deeply held belief was firmly established when I arrived at school and I was unconsciously giving out those signals to the other children around me. Those children who had similar or worse experiences than mine, recognised this similar suffering in me and became my friends. Other children who came from a stronger sense of themselves tended to view me and people like me, as a point of ridicule and humiliation; someone to be pushed around.

In my story, these beliefs were to be even more deeply embedded by the unfortunate choice of my first teacher. Far from seeing her work as a vocation and motivated by a love of children, our first-grade teacher seemed to be the most vindictive person imaginable. Even now, with all the years of experience since those early events, I find it hard to recall anyone else I have ever met who has displayed such extraordinary levels of cruelty.

She found the need to imprint her own internal pain on her pupils through physical punishment and public humiliation. A favourite trick of hers was to make a child who had wet themselves in class - probably because she had refused them permission to go to the toilet - stand up on a chair for the rest of the lesson so everyone knew how dirty he or

Chapter 1: My Story

she was. This was in the reception class of four and five-year-old children. It seems extraordinary in this day and age to imagine such behaviour and yet she was merely a product of her time. The understanding of a child-centred education was many decades away.

The cruelty I experienced at school was only matched by the chaos at home. My mother was barely able to cope from one day to the next. My father was mostly absent. My older siblings were either constantly fighting, or stayed away from the house and my Autistic sister, Bernie and myself, were left to our own devices for much of the time.

By the time I had reached secondary school, I had hardened up and become more street-wise. I had built up my own resilience, by creating a brash outer shell, which was near impossible to breach. I learnt to keep my head down, keep out of trouble, or fight my way out, if backed into a corner.

School, even by the tender age of eleven was no longer something I could take seriously. It was something to be endured until I could get away from this life. Everything became one big joke and I found it easier to laugh and fool around than to look deeper into the pain in my heart.

At the time it just seemed like survival, but looking back, I can see a much deeper wisdom at play. Somewhere deep inside me there was a quiet whisper encouraging me to see a way through the madness by not taking life too seriously and to hold on to the belief; *'things will get better.'*

Although I survived the school years pretty well and formed a good group of friends around me, my interest in education was never ignited and I left school with no qualifications and no plan of what I was going to do. I did not come from a background were education was highly valued. The only expectations from my parents were to do the same as they had done and readily accept low skilled and low paid work.

Early adulthood

I left home at aged 18 and tried a variety of administration and reception jobs in the first few years. With no real plan or direction in my life, I fell into a short-term and hedonistic pattern of waiting to be paid at the end of the week and drinking heavily for most of the weekend. I would not describe

Chapter 1: My Story

these years as difficult; in fact they were, at times, a lot of fun, but I did have a nagging feeling there was more to life than this.

At some point, I gave the nagging feeling enough space to emerge and bring forth a moment of clarity, which was to prove pivotal to my life. I knew in my heart the pattern and way of life I was living was destructive and would lead me nowhere. I knew at a deeper level if I wanted to change my life I had to change the circumstances of my life. Looking back later, I realised this was the first great lesson of my life. Within a few months of this realisation, I had moved out of Birmingham and accepted a live-in position, at a country hotel in Somerset.

We can all learn from these life lessons and it does not have to be as dramatic as this for everyone. For me, everything had to change; my job, my home, my friends and my environment. For other people, it might be a subtler shift in life circumstances, which can bring about a positive change. However, we can never expect change to occur when everything around us stays the same. We need to find a way through to new paths, new patterns and space for new thinking to emerge. Albert Einstein[1] famously said:

*"The definition of insanity is doing
the same thing over
and over again and expecting a different result."*

This can be very true of our own lives. If everything around us stays the same, how can we expect a different result for ourselves?

The move to the country agreed with me and it is probably no accident I have lived in or close to the countryside ever since. The beauty of Somerset charmed me, but it was the magnificence of the Cotswolds which really took my breath away and would play a big part in my later adult life.

Finding love

The area of the Cotswolds is a series of market towns and villages nestled in-between Cheltenham, Oxford and Stratford-upon-Avon. They are numerous but all have a distinct charm of honey-coloured stone cottages, which transport you back to an idyllic pre-industrial age. In this beautiful and tranquil place, I started to open up like a flower.

Chapter 1: My Story

Such beautiful surroundings had a profound impact on my sense of wellbeing. I started to feel peaceful and at home, probably for the first time in my life.

I was still brash and crude. The street urchin had not completely left me, but there were new and subtler aspects of my personality starting to emerge. Perhaps because of this and the change in my energy and my psyche, I became open to and eventually welcomed love into my life.

However, love didn't come into my life in quite the way I had expected, but arrived in the form of a gentle loving person who was the chef in the hotel where I was working. That person also happened to be female. The road to true love as they say does not run easy and this was certainly true for me. I had been at battle with myself and the world around me for so long that of course I didn't simply put down my arms and let peace convene in this newfound state. I still had doubts and uncertainties about myself and about the nature of the relationship I was entering into, given its unconventional path. But I could see the prize beyond the fears and I kept my faith that this was the right thing for me.

Coming Home to You

Obstacles and interferences also came from those around us, who judged and railed against our choice. This helped to solidify rather than undermine our commitment to each other. Many important life lessons came from this time in my life and from the choices I made. Perhaps the biggest and most important decision was to welcome love into my life in whatever form it presented itself, regardless of whether it was acceptable to anyone else around me. I learnt love really does know no boundaries. It is only ourselves who create them. Once we let go of our mistaken beliefs and our need for other people's approval, we can find our way in the world and magical things will start to happen.

Despite losing friends, a job, a home linked to the job and almost losing all family contact, still the resolve that this was the right decision for me never wavered. One of the most pivotal points in my life was the conversation with my parents about this relationship. When my mother served an ultimatum, saying, *"It's her or us",* I found it easy and natural to say, *"It is her. It will always be her, for she is love. I choose love."* Although only 21 at the time, I knew this was a defining moment of choosing not only love,

10

but the quality of love I wanted in my life, even if it meant breaking familial ties.

We do not always get the love we want or deserve from those we believe are closest to us. When we understand deeply the difference between love and duty, we see that love leads us to happiness and duty ties us down with binds of suffering. We are all free to make the best choices for ourselves. My parent's ultimatum helped me to realise I felt no duty to them beyond respecting the role they had played in my life up until that point. If we had now reached a point where we had to go our separate ways, I could accept this and go peacefully, wishing them well. In the end, my mother saw my resolve and already had plenty of experience of my strength of character, to know I would not change my mind. So an uneasy truce was formed.

From this experience came another important life lesson, the importance of courage. Our soul is made up of the purest energy imaginable. It is clear about what it needs and when you listen to it carefully and follow its gentle guidance it will literally sing to you. This is what happiness feels like; our soul sings to us. The path the soul will guide us down may not be the one which we thought we would follow, or the one other people would have us follow, but it will never be a wrong choice. It will always lead to something amazing in the end. But to follow the soul's whisper takes courage. When we stand up for what we believe is right for ourselves, there are always consequences. What I've learnt over the years is that people fear this kind of courage. They fear the connection we are able to make with our own heart and soul, because it can show them how disconnected they feel to theirs. This is not understood at a conscious level, yet it plays out in the energy and dynamics of our relationships. When I listened to my soul's whispers and chose love over convention, I found many people judged and condemned my actions, but there were others who supported us. I was powered by an inner resolve, knowing this was the right choice for me and I would cope with the fallout. In the end, it proved so and Joy my partner and I are still happily together nearly 30 years later. Still living our life, our way, supporting each other and feeling the same vibrant love, which was sparked all those years ago.

New directions

The choice of this new and unexpected relationship opened new paths and directions in my life, which I would never have dreamed of before. We moved back to Joy's hometown in Yorkshire and from this stable base I returned to education, initially retaking my O'level Examinations and then I went on to university. More importantly, it sparked a thirst for knowledge, which has never left me. I found I had a passion for education and the new doors it can open. It was as if a veil had been lifted and suddenly life had a new and more expanded view to show me.

I started a career in Social Work and became qualified while working with families in crisis and dealing with cases of severe child abuse. Witnessing the traumas people find themselves in, or the intentional actions of family members to cause harm to their most vulnerable members, helped to shape much of my philosophical beliefs and deep compassion for the world. The scale and breadth of the hardships, depravity and cruelty was pretty tough to deal with, but I knew I could only focus on what I could give to the situation right at that moment. I could not change the past and I could do little to influence the future. I focused on the support, kindness and love I could bring to those in need of my help. This focus has never left me and is part of what people recognise as my compassionate and loving nature. By being exposed to some of the horrors of modern living, I was able to find my own humanity and I have remained open-hearted ever since, no matter how overwhelming the circumstances. Hate and judgement do not transform anything, they only allow us to vent our anger and often force the offending actions underground. If we want to transform the ills of our modern society, we have to do it with an open heart, acceptance and love.

I stayed in social work for six years, before moving in to the management of care services, specialising in the support for adults with Autism. When I felt I had reached all I could in this field, I moved on to management consultancy, working with multinationals on their change needs. It sounds like a big jump from being a social worker to becoming a consultant and of course there was some further study involved, but for me it was a natural progression. I continued to work with people who felt lost, vulnerable, afraid and in need of gentle

Chapter 1: My Story

guidance to put them on the right path again. The situations and the problems were different, but the basic human needs for support, acceptance and kindness were the same.

I continued to flourish in the world of business, setting up my own consultancy, yet I felt I was failing to hear my inner voice and notice my inner world. I moved from contract to contract, solving one problem, moving to another, with little reflection of either the experience, myself or any greater tapestry of life I was operating within.

It was at the apparent peak of my career when it all started to unravel. The greater organising universe had plans for me and if I was not going to listen to the gentle nudges and pangs of intuition, which emerged every now and again, I was going to receive a great big shove in the right direction. I was brought down by illness. Many people see illness as a curse and of course, when it happened to me I was not celebrating. But illness when viewed mindfully can really help us to slow down and take stock of our lives. If the very life energy we take for granted, which allows us to rush around and busy up our lives has been taken away, we only have the present moment to contemplate our situation.

Coming Home to You

It doesn't matter what name the illness has, it will still allow the same thing to occur. For us to slow down and weigh up our life's choices and to consider whether these are a reflection of our life's purpose. For me, it was a parasitic bug in my digestive system, which slowly unravelled my whole immune system. Bit by bit, I had to learn to slow down, accept the pain and discomfort and start to learn how to communicate with my body and ultimately, with my inner self. After feeling completely let down by the traditional medical profession, an integrative health practitioner (trained in traditional and alternative healing methods) performed an energy clearing ritual for me and it subtly started to change my situation. Slowly, I found my way back to full health, which took more than a year, but far more importantly, I changed my mindset. I started to question far more deeply what was going on in my inner world and what I could learn from it. Up until this point, I had been obsessed with books, facts and figures and believed all knowledge came from the known world, the external world. I suddenly started to realise there was a world of wisdom and learning to tap into within our very selves. It was an earth-shattering realisation, which changed my whole perspective on life.

I understood the need to see beyond the physical world. When we only focus on the physical body and the material world, we limit our horizons and prevent ourselves from becoming whole, happy and healthy.

One of the greatest realisations I made at this time, which would shape the rest of my life, was the understanding that we are all energy. Beyond the illusion of the body and of physical separation from one and other, there is unifying, intelligent energy, as Einstein described it which binds us all to this huge tapestry called life. Understanding this unifying energy and its underlying intelligence became my life's focus. I wanted to learn to use it for my benefit and for the benefit of other people.

The journey within

Around this time, I started meditating. Nobody was more surprised than myself, who had up until this point lived my life at full tilt, forever going on to the next experience and the next, with little time for consolidation or reflection. One day I simply felt this nudge to give it a go. I was not calm or quiet enough to go and sit quietly by myself so I started with guided meditations, which are freely available on YouTube. I listened at the start or end of my day, with little clear intent involved, but after settling into the daily practice, it quickly became a mainstay of my life. I moved on from guided meditations to silent sessions, where I found my connection with a deeper more up-lifting energy, which grew with each session. I started to receive messages and images in these meditations, which impacted positively on my life. I made changes to my diet - focusing on wholesome nutritious food - and worked on my posture and attitude toward my body.

Some years later, during a particularly deep meditation session I had a profound experience of communication with my non-verbal Autistic sister, Bernie. She had lived in a small community home for more than 25 years. Although her physical needs were taken care of, she had shown in many ways she was deeply unhappy, through her constant screaming and occasional head banging and violence towards other people. During my morning meditation one day, Bernie and I had a communication, a conversation. This happened at what I can only describe as an energetic level. It was not like a dream when you have a scene played out, it was far more intimate and real. I was also fully conscious and able to ask questions and influence the conversation, something which rarely happens in a dream-state.

During our conversation, I learnt that Bernie, who was 47 by then, was getting ready to leave this world. She told me her purpose here had gone as far as it could go. It has not been fully realised and she needed to move on. Her 'soul' contract with me had been fulfilled and she described the beauty and love of our connection in a way I can never fully express in words. As devastating as the news was to hear, I was able to calmly accept it. It came from such a deep place of honesty and connection. I could not do otherwise.

Sure enough in the weeks which followed I watched Bernie's health deteriorate. I saw the ineptitude of the medics in dealing with Bernie effectively in a hospital setting or to fully diagnose the cancer. I watched her agonising in pain and found that the staff were unable or unwilling to appreciate her discomfort. To their untrained eye - in observing someone with Autism deal with pain - she was fine. As traumatic as it was to go through the hospital system and the poor care being dispensed all around us, I held onto the clear connection and the message Bernie had given me. I was not trying to deny her imminent death or blame anyone for her condition, only to ensure she received good end-of-life care and did not suffer unnecessarily.

I was there to be with Bernie, to advocate her needs and ensure her dying wish was fulfilled - her wish to die at home in her own bed with her own people around her. It was sixteen weeks from the initial communication with Bernie until the time she passed away.

I felt guided by a greater force all through the weeks, which unfolded and particularly the last week, when I was with her in the hospital and in the final night I stayed with her at her home. I understood at a much deeper level than I ever had before, how we are all connected to this greater tapestry called life. The nature of death is only a move into our spirit selves - a return to our essential nature - rather than the end. A luminary of our age, Wayne Dyer[2] said:

"We are Spiritual beings having a temporal experience in a physical body."

Despite the deep grief, which enfolded me when Bernie had passed away, it brought a whole new perspective on life, the universe and our place in this magical world. I learnt that once this door of understanding has opened it simply cannot be closed again. What exists always exists. Truth is eternal and will guide us through our darkest days back to the light. Once I had experienced such a profound experience, bringing messages of such great importance, I became aware of the messages all around me in every shape and form, simply waiting for me to notice them.

Through my own grieving process and my journey back to wholeness, I realised we are not here to deny or rail against the pain of loss, but to accept it; to observe its impact and to know the heart will always move to heal our hurt if we allow it. The purpose of life is not to avoid pain, seeking only pleasure. The purpose of life is to embrace every aspect of it, to learn to accept, understand and to experience both the good and the difficult.

Bernie left me with an amazing gift. As well as the beautiful subtle connection and love we shared, she helped me to listen more carefully to the signs, whispers and nudges which life is sending me all the time. She taught me to trust in the greater unifying force all around us and by giving my faith to this, rather than my ego mind, I have found greater peace and happiness than I ever thought possible. She taught me to believe in the beauty of life as it unfolds around us. When I learnt to keep my intent pure and focused on the greater good, life would always bring me what I needed, because it can do nothing else. Its purpose is to support our true purpose. The greater universal force is here to serves us all. I realised that a quiet mind and a separation of the inner self, from the ego mind, were essential for my spiritual growth.

My deeper twice-daily meditation practises as they had become, had a profound effect on me. Outwardly I became calm, settled, joyful and more effective in every aspect of my life. Business projects became easier, despite working in more demanding and dysfunctional organisations.

I could see my contribution as part of a bigger picture and I no longer became embroiled in the everyday dramas around me. Inwardly, I became much more aware of my energy source, my conscious influence on my body and its functioning. I became aware of the thoughts popping into my head which were mere distractions and not helpful to me.

This is the journey of discovery I would like to take you on. The journey to the most fascinating

Chapter 1: My Story

landscape you will ever discover; the journey to the centre of you. In *Coming Home to You*, we will delve into the centre of ourselves and experience the limitless horizons of discovery, which dwell within us all. The closer we believe we are to a boundary, a border or a limitation, the more we will find new ground and territory to explore; a world without end.

In connecting to our infinite nature, we connect with the pure essence of who we are. We connect to the essence in all of life. A conscious entity, which animates all of life in this world, but is not part of it. It is a conscious being, which inhabits our body, but is not limited or defined by it.

And as we make deeper connections with our inward nature, into the very soul of our being, we learn the truth, which sets us free. We can come home to ourselves.

"Change is not something to be fearful of,
in fact the opposite is true.
We should always be suspicious of stagnation
and the loss of movement in our life."

Chapter 2

What is the Nature of Change

Change is the only constant in life and yet it is the one concept many of us struggle to accept. We try to plan, control and anticipate, in our need to avoid accepting change. Our modern times have given us the illusion that we can control everything in our environment. But it has also taken away the one thing that has enabled us to become the most successful species on this planet; our ability to adapt. Once we learn to embrace change and all the learning which comes with it, we can live a fulfilled and happy life, full of adventures and possibilities.

In this chapter we will explore:

☑ *the nature of change;*

☑ *how change affects us;*

☑ *how to embrace acceptance; and*

☑ *how to develop new beliefs about change.*

Change is all around us

Change of any sort is a challenge to us. As humans, we have evolved through a tightrope balance of cat and mouse. At times we were the mouse and at other times the cat. Through thousands of years of cumulative experience, we have learnt like all other mammal species to be observant and suspicious of unexpected changes in our environment.

Another evolution alongside this instinctive response is that of our frontal lobe brain, which has grown significantly out of proportion to our fellow mammals. This is the part of our brain which gives us the anticipatory thinking modes as well as a deep and detailed retention-thinking mode. It has allowed humans to become the single dominant species of the planet in terms of controlling and managing our external environment.

This sense of control is only illusionary, since of course we have no control over the weather, over natural forces such as earthquakes and volcanoes and of course over lunar, solar and planetary activity which affects the earth's activities. However, if we simply park this major 'but' for a moment, humans have the illusion of control of our world and this has allowed us to develop one thing no other species appears to have developed; an ego.

The nature of ego

What exactly is an ego you might ask? Well it's an interesting question with no easy answer. At its simplest form, it is a reaction machine inside our head, evolving from our primitive brain into a superstar story telling machine. For example, if you are in a dark alley at night and you hear a rustle behind you, your primitive brain immediately notices the noise and slows down all other cognitive abilities to assess and decide what course of action is needed. This is done in milliseconds. Far more than our modern cognitive brain can achieve, our primitive brain will take in all the current surrounding information on the terrain, the options for quick escape, the potential for a dangerous presence and trawl through past information for similar situations it can draw on; so far, so mammal.

The ego mind can add another layer of drama to the situation. It will be able to go through hundreds, if not thousands of potential reasons for the noise. These can be in the bad camp – 'mass murderer' or 'rapist'. Or they can be in the good camp – 'oh has Jenny caught me up at last, I was wondering where she was!' The point is, this scenario-creating machine is what separates us from our fellow mammals.

Not only is the ego mind a most imaginative article, it also has the ability to generate fear. Now all mammals have the ability to generate fear, but for most mammals this is often instantaneous, based on a definite stimulus and it is immediately released once the situation has returned to safety. But for us humans this is less straightforward. The ego can continue to play out scenarios, options, near misses and potential near misses in our mind repetitively. This can keep us in a fear loop for hours, if not constantly playing out at a low level.

Immediately we have a dilemma, as our advanced and highly evolved brains which are intelligent, intuitive and innovative come with the potential handicap of the ego. I say potentially since there are significant portions of our species, which have been able to override the most debilitating aspects of the ego and use it to bring heights of creativity and engineering to our world. But at the other extreme, it has also brought huge devastation, tragedy and conflict.

This does not mean the news is bad, or that our ego is our enemy. Quite the opposite in fact, it is a natural part of our evolution, which has allowed us to access higher levels of conscious intent than any other species on the planet as far as we are aware. But the ego is not us, only a part of us. It is important to place it in the right position as a support function, but this can be easier said than done.

Nowhere, does this become particularly truer than when we face change. It fires up the ego to go into overdrive and allows our fear muscles to come to the fore. The fact is, change is neither good nor bad. It just is. Like winter follows fall, and spring follows winter, there is nothing we can do about it but prepare and accept the changes. After all, we are on a planet, which is spinning around a burning star in an ever-expanding universe. There is no one moment, which is the same as the next. Only an ego, obsessed with control, can believe we have any real influence on our environment.

If our role is not to resist change or to control or stop it, what should we do? Accept it! Only when we can accept it can we move on to see new possibilities which can emerge.

The change roller coaster

When we are facing change, particularly major change, it fires up many emotions, as we come to terms with the implications. Depending on the nature of change and our reaction to it, this can be a very quick affair, over within a matter of minutes or hours, or in the case of grief it can take several years to process the many emotions which may arise. This roller coaster of emotions is often described as a change curve and looks something like the diagram below.

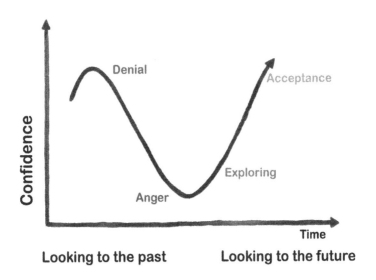

The model originates from Dr Elisabeth Kübler-Ross[3] who in 1969, identified the five stages of grief. The diagram above is closer to the more general change model designed by John Fisher in 2002, based on the similar roller coaster of emotions we experience during any change situation. Once we are through the initial shock of hearing about the change we descend into anger or despair before gradually lifting. Recognising the process of change is one of the ways we can be helped through it and I frequently use this model in my work on organisational change.

When we say, life is a roller-coaster, we are literally and figuratively acknowledging the ups and downs of our emotions, which we go through in life. We cannot avoid these highs and lows, or even the circumstances, which trigger these responses. But we can learn to become more observant of our reactions and learn to consciously move through them in a more gentle and loving manner.

This requires a different relationship to our ego and the fear it generates when we go through these cycles. The change may be big – such as the loss of a loved one – or it may be small like having to change where our desk is located in our workplace. Either one will trigger the cycle. The difference is the depth of trauma experienced and the time to work through the cycle will differ tremendously based on the size of the change we are experiencing.

The two factors of change

In all of my experiences in helping individuals and organisations manage change, there are two common factors which make the biggest difference in how well a person can move through these cycles and get out of the trauma and fear patterns which dominate in this period.

The first is belief. It is the belief that the result at the other end will lead to a return to calmness, happiness and equilibrium. Notice I do not say, a return to normal, since it is very unlikely. Once we have gone through a change we are never the same again. But this is exactly the point. We are not meant to be the same again, we are meant to have grown, to have experienced and to have reached a new understanding as a result of the change. Evolution is a constant force and we are as much at its behest now as we have ever been. We are on a constant cycle of growth and adaption, which will never cease.

The second is acceptance. This is a particularly tough one to get our heads around, especially when we are facing major challenges such as a sudden death of a child or the slow decline of a loved one. However, we need to think of what the flip side of this is and what it does to us. Non-acceptance, no matter how much we may believe it helps us to avoid feeling the pain of our circumstances, instead brings us suffering. It drives us to use our own internal energy to fight with the world and say; *"This cannot be happening to me? I won't accept this! This cannot be!"*

Chapter 2: What is the Nature of Change

But this is our ego voice. The one which drives us to believe our experience is unique, when in fact there will be tens of thousands of other people experiencing exactly what we are experiencing in that moment.

Viktor Frankl was a holocaust survivor who became an esteemed psychiatrist after the war. When he wrote of his experiences in the concentration camps of Nazi Germany, he became an inspiration to millions of people, showing as he did, the extent we are capable of accepting our circumstances and how we can learn to keep our heart and our mind open to possibilities. He wrote of the horrors he witnessed, of the overwhelming losses of everyone he loved. Yet his quest, even in the midst of the horrors, was to not lose his sense of humanity and dignity. In his book *A Search for Meaning*[4] he said:

> *"In a position of utter desolation, when man cannot express himself in positive action, when his only achievement may consist of enduring his suffering in the right way – an honourable way – in such a position man can, through loving contemplation of the image he carries of his beloved, achieve fulfilment"*

Coming Home to You

As difficult as acceptance is to achieve in the face of overwhelming grief, it's a walk in the park in comparison to the non-acceptance we often take in response to personal and societal traumas. When we are in a cycle of non-acceptance, we are effectively going to war with ourselves. We start using our ego to define all sorts of scenarios and situations, which might play out. We start using our energies to assign blame to everyone who might have had a hand in the situation, including apportioning a large part of the blame to ourselves. We use our energy to build a campaign of action to right the wrong in some way. This gives us the illusion that we are moving away from the point of the pain, but it does not move us towards a point of healing. In truth, it is likely to keep us in a cycle of grief, suffering and anger for a longer time.

All of this non-acceptance also keeps us in a place of non-reality. We have moved ourselves, our ego and our energy from a place where we can really see things for what they are. We start building a picture of life built on the sense of injustice, anger and denial we are holding in our hearts. How can such a foundation ever move us towards a place of healing? From this viewpoint, we start to forget the reality that the moment of the tragedy has in fact already passed. We play it again and again in our own mind, looking at it from every angle and putting ourselves in the starring role assigning blame to ourselves for not avoiding the trauma in the first place. We have moved ourselves so far from reality at this point nothing can be seen in its right proportion. Even the very person or instance, which triggered the change becomes more distance because we have built a picture of our thoughts around the situation, rather than staying open to the learning which the changes can bring.

As difficult and painful as acceptance is, it is nothing in comparison to the hardship and suffering which will be felt on the path of non-acceptance.

Embracing change

Change is something we can ignore, but we cannot avoid forever. Understanding that our true nature is a constant flow of energy, which is moving and changing with the tides of life, can help us to embrace change. One of the simplest ways we can learn to embrace change is to connect with our breath.

37

No one breath is the same as another and no one breath can be held onto longer than the body needs it. We do not mourn the passing of one breath, because we know there is another one coming along right after it. We do not store our breaths, for fear of running out. At some point, the body's wisdom will take over and release it, reassuring us it will take another breath when we need it.

Embracing change can be viewed in much the same way. Storing our fears, memories and traumas is like holding on to old and unwanted energy. It does not serve us and leaves little space for new and positive experiences to come our way. When we allow our breath to flow freely, we place trust in life supporting us and delivering what we need, when we need it. When we extend this trust to the greater pattern of life we are living freely, knowing we will always be supported, no matter how hard the change feels. When we learn to embrace change, and allow it to lead us where it will, life becomes the adventure it was always meant to be.

 **Call to action**

Change is not something to be fearful of, in fact the opposite is true. We should always be suspicious of stagnation and the loss of movement in our life. Change is like a muscle, which we can build and flex over time. It requires a mindset in sync with the flow of life all around us. There is no aspect of life, which stays the same from one moment to the next. Each tree, each flower, each creature and even the cells in our own body are in a constant state of flux. When we understand the value of living in the present moment, not regretting the past, or becoming anxious of the future, we can embrace the joy of change. Instead of damming up the flow of change which abounds all around us, like a river running dry, we can learn to let it flow and in doing so, we reveal the magic which abounds all around us.

 **Make it happen**

In this, and each subsequent section at the end of the chapter there are several practical exercises you can try. Each is designed to help you address the issues discussed in the chapter and develop helpful habits to support your transformation journey.

In this section, there are three exercises. They can be done together, or you can choose the one that most resonates with you. Using a journal is one of the most powerful ways we can build our inner life and you will see this suggestion is repeated in later chapters. If you do not own a suitable notebook, I encourage you to find a robust, lightweight and well-designed notebook you can take with you wherever you go.

1. Start to make mental notes every day of situations where you have no control over and how well you cope with the changes.

   For example, the weather, your commute to work, the reliability of public transport, a friend's mood when you meet them for a drink. The list goes on and on. *Start to flex your change muscle.*

2. Learn to accept circumstances that did not end well for you.

   Think of a time when something did not go the way you wanted. It can be something big or small. For example, having an argument with a colleague, missing an important meeting, or having to cancel a holiday due to family illness. Whatever it was, think of the result. What do you perceive as the down side of that 'miss' in your life and what are the potential upsides? Write down the things that changed as a result of the situation, noting both the upsides and the downsides. Taking time to reflect on a disappointment helps you to see there were other important things that could only happen as a result of this situation.

3. Write down one of the biggest regrets in your life.

Describe what you had been expecting as an outcome. Compare it with your life now. Note the things that are less satisfying now as a result of this regret, but also, note the areas that feel better. Take time to review your notes and review how big the regret feels to you now. Remember all of life brings ups and downs. No one can go through life without experiencing loss and disappointment. The loss itself may help you to learn, reflect, experience and grow. All loss and regret add meaning to our life, once we know how to reflect and understand their true nature better.

"Once we make the break between who
we are and the emotion we feel,
we become free. Our psyche and energy
becomes peaceful and we start to see
something amazing happen.
We feel joy and happiness rise within us."

CHAPTER 3

Control Your Emotions, Control Your Life

Our emotions have a huge impact on the quality of our life. When we feel good, life feels good. When we are sad or depressed, life can feel like a prison. Learning to control our emotions is one of the most effective ways to find happiness, not because we force ourselves to be positive, but because we are no longer enslaved by the whims of our emotions. We can break out of our self-imposed prison by learning to observe and change our emotions.

In this chapter, we will explore:

- ☑ *the difference between emotions and ourselves;*

- ☑ *emotions as part of the ever-present energy field all around us;*

- ☑ *how to tap into and unblock our energy; and*

- ☑ *how to create distance and choice around our emotions through observation.*

The Power of Emotions

When I was growing up I had a fiery temper, which was ignited by the smallest of things. For example, somebody calling me a name, not getting my favourite dish for dinner, or feeling too hot and not being able to undo the buttons of my coat quickly enough; small things which incited a big reaction. I was not an unpleasant child, many people described me as kind and thoughtful, but when something happened that I couldn't accept, then my meltdown overshadowed any of the more noble emotions I held within.

My environment shaped many of my reactions. I observed from a very young age the angry, hurtful and unguarded exchanges between my parents and siblings. Being free with my tongue and careless with my thoughts was a way of life for me. It was based on my experiences and from my limited viewpoint I believed it was the way most families behaved. Exchanges in our house often led to shouting and screaming at each other and saying very unkind and cruel things. In retrospect, I see how damaging this was to all of us in the household. And for me, it led to unhealthy patterns of dealing with and suppressing emotions.

45

Coming Home to You

What I know now is that emotions are very powerful. They have huge energy behind them and when expressed negatively, can be very damaging to our relationships. When I left home and started out for myself, I learned through my work, friendships and general experiences that expressing emotions could not be done freely, or unguardedly because this led to negative consequences, such as the loss of a friendship or difficult relations with work colleagues. I learned to reign in my reactions and think about what I wanted to express before speaking. As my career progressed and I had more senior roles, I was able to keep a calm exterior even if the negative emotions were being played out somewhere in my mind. This separation of internal thoughts and external actions helped me to become very successful in my career, even under intense work pressure, I was viewed as reliable, calm and usually described as fun to work with. However, happiness did not flow from this success, because I continued to have an internal script playing out in my head, one of annoyance, anger and fear. Although I was polite and engaging with my teams or clients, there was always a frustration building inside me, due to some internal dialogue or set of beliefs I was holding.

What I did not appreciate is that even if I didn't express these negative emotions, they were still playing into the dynamic of my interactions with other people. When my internal emotions were ones of frustration, anger or annoyance, it impacted on the experiences and impressions created by the people around me, whether I interacted with them or not. They picked up some underlying discomfort or frustration, which was in the air so to speak, even if it was not expressed directly. In many of my dealings with people I left some residual annoyance, doubt or frustration.

Emotions I now understand have their own energy. The power of this energy can be a force for attraction or can be repellent, which is why we can have such strong reactions to people around us, even if we have not spoken to them directly. In a public place, or walking into a room in the heat of an argument, even if the people involved have stopped mid-flow on our arrival, we are immediately able to pick up on the tense and strained atmosphere their emotions have created.

The reason for this is that each emotion we express has a unique vibration or signature of its own. Emotions are energy waves, expressed from our own energetic field and each has a distinctive length and frequency. Some of these we create from our own actions, thoughts and stimulus and some we pick up from the world around us. The interplay between our emotions and those that are in the atmosphere around us is very subtle yet has a profound impact on our life and relationships. When we are carrying around emotions of anger, grief, rage and despair, even if we are not sharing them openly with others, they will be touching and affecting every interaction we have.

Emotions are not our enemy and we are not trying to stop our emotions from being expressed. They allow us to experience life to the fullest. The broad spectrum of emotions we feel and express are part of our evolutionary path. They have helped us to survive in the world, build complex social structures, be more curious, more creative and more engaged with the act of life, as we have grown as individuals and indeed as a species. Emotions can play a very important role in our growth and development. The hot emotions of love, anger and passion drive us forward and can be the most important motivators as we discover our life path. The cold emotions of rage, grief and depression can literally stop us in our tracks and keep us stuck in a very dark place for a long time.

Emotions come at a cost, feeding off our own energy source to be launched into an expression of their own. This energy that fuels our emotions comes from the same reserves that allows us to live, breathe and enjoy life. When we have emotional highs and lows in our life, we quite literally feel exhausted because they have drained our energy tank. Learning to manage our emotions is an important step in learning to live a balanced and harmonious life.

Smoothing out the roller-coaster of life to have a steady flow of energy available to us, leads to a much more enjoyable and peaceful life. This happened for me when I started to separate out my sense of self from my emotions. I discovered that when I could see emotions emerging and question their source and validity, they were able to dissipate much quicker, no longer taking hold of my mind and energy. What I started to see in my interactions with friends, family and colleagues was a flow and ease that had not been there before. I literally felt lighter in myself and every situation felt easier. I no longer saw conflict and challenges around me, only opportunities to learn and grow. This transformed my relationships into gentle, easy-going and enjoyable exchanges. At work, even the most challenging project was fun and engaging. At home, my friendships and interactions with my life partner became deeper, more loving and more authentic. I felt as if I had returned home to myself. The additional effect of observing and releasing my emotions in a more conscious way allowed my energy levels to stabilise. I no longer had the highs and lows, which had been the pattern of my life and I felt a constant flow of energy around me, which has never left me. When we learn to observe, understand and manage our emotions, it brings many positive impacts. Perhaps one of the most important is it can bring tranquillity and happiness to every day of our life.

How to observe your emotions

The first step in understanding and controlling your emotions is learning to observe them. When I was younger, I believed I was the emotion I was expressing in that moment. I completely identified with my anger, frustration, happiness, or whatever it was. I was not unique in this over-identification with the emotion, since we are all brought up to believe this, to some degree.

Learning to separate our emotion from ourselves is one of the first steps in transforming our emotional health. When we start to observe, it feels quite alien and the insights might only stay for a short while and arise some time after the emotion has been expressed. Over time, these moments of insight and observation can become longer and occur while the emotion is being expressed, allowing us to interact with it more directly and change its impact and direction mid-flow.

Becoming the objective observer of our emotions as they arise allows us to bring perspective and also gives us choice. The most important choice is whether we wish to identify with this emotion. After all, emotions are simply energy waves passing through us. In another moment, there will be another energy wave, why do we want to grab and hold on to this one? A simple thing you can do is to start questioning the nature of the emotions you are feeling. For example, when you find yourself calming down from an emotional outburst, look at the nature of the emotion you have expressed and where you felt it in your body. Ask yourself if the emotion was really to do with the situation that triggered it, or whether it was linked to something deeper that has not yet been expressed.

All emotions bring a cost with them in terms of our own energy levels and the health of our psyche. When we give those emotions to other people in an unguarded and thoughtless way, we are actually giving away our very life force. In some cases, and for some relationships this is exactly our intent. When we express the feelings of love and compassion we have an unending supply of energy, which will pour through us and we can directly give it to the object of our attention.

When we give away negative emotions such as fear, anger and hate, we are simply draining the life from ourselves and giving it to someone else. The reason these emotions are draining is because they suck energy out of us and do not naturally replenish themselves. In one moment of expression, we have literally given our life away. If you observe this happening to you, the question to ask yourself is; did this person or situation deserve to take my life force away from me?

Once I started to observe my emotions more clearly and question their source and reason, it became much easier to identify and release them naturally through gentle reflection. This turned around every aspect of my life including the interactions with colleagues, friends and loved ones. Once we make the break between who we are and the emotion we feel, we become free. Our psyche and energy becomes peaceful and we start to see something amazing happen. We feel joy and happiness rise in us. Not the kind of joy and happiness associated with an event or seeing a beloved friend, but a deeper, subtler and more sustaining joy which is always in the background. It never leaves us and is always there, waiting to be discovered.

You have the power to change your world by changing how you view, interpret and act on your emotions. The first step is to make your emotions your friend rather than your enemy. Emotions simply exist, like the sky and the moon exist. Emotions are not good or bad. What they do is allow us to key in to something deeper, which is going on, in ourselves and in the world around us. They are our signposts for taking a deeper note of what is happening and what we can learn from it.

Anger can be a great force for overcoming injustices if we use it wisely. Fear can help us to understand what we are suppressing or denying in ourselves and act as a signpost for our personal growth. Grief can allow us to reflect and understand when something important has passed away and what it meant to us. Love brings connection and meaning into our life. All emotions will change in time and when we learn to notice them as they arise, look within ourselves to what they mean or point to in us, we are able to act with clear and positive intent.

Managing and clearing emotions in our daily lives is vitally important to our physical health because they can cause imbalances and blockages in the body. If we have had a traumatic event, which has triggered fear and we have associated ourselves with this emotion it will manifest in the upper chest area, literally affecting our ability to breathe.

If we allow our anger or injustice to turn to rage, it will be felt as a cold hard feeling in the pit of our stomach, often causing digestion issues. We are unable to digest anything in life if the energy of rage has blocked our digestive system.

If we have closed our heart to love, we can find it manifesting itself as physical blockages, as the energy of isolation we have created will start to affect the heart and its surrounding area.

Unblock your emotions

There is a fundamental split between Eastern and Western philosophies about how the body, health and healing are viewed. The West is heavily influenced by the work of Hippocrates, a Greek from the 5th century who taught medicine based on observable phenomena in the body, such as physical symptoms and bodily fluids.

In the East, Chinese and Indian medicine focuses on both observable and unobservable phenomena, including energy. This distinction between the two schools of thought shows in their modern equivalent practices. In the West, we often used pharmaceutical based drugs for treatment. In the East, they use a mixture of energy work such as acupuncture or acupressure and herbal medicines.

It is the recognition of energy and its importance to our health, which signposts the importance of releasing energy to restore health. We do not have to live with blocked emotions in our body, we have many ways to unblock them. Two relatively recent techniques that have emerged involve using energy points on the body and a set of words or phrases to release emotions.

The first technique is The Healing Code by Alex Lloyd, PhD and Ben Johnson, MD[5]. It works on energy and using key focus points around the head, whilst reciting a mantra. As you bring your fingers to rest over the key areas you recite the following:

"I ask that all known and unknown hidden beliefs, destructive cellular memories and all physical ailments in relation to [name of problem] are found, opened and healed, by filling me with

the love, life and light of God [the universe, the unifying field, or whatever divine presence you recognise]. I ask that the power of this healing is increased by one hundred times or more."

The four healing centres are shown in the diagram below.

The four healing centres

1. Bridge Position

This healing centre is located between the eyebrows

2. Adam's Apple Position

Resting your arms on your chest, aim your fingertips at the base your throat

3. Jaw Position

Aim your fingertips at the bottom back corner of your jawbone under your ear

4. Temples Position

Aim your fingertips at the temple area

The second technique, which has many similarities to the first is the Emotional Freedom Technique, which was developed by Gary Craig in his seminal work *The EFT Manual* and more recently popularised by Nick Ortner[6] in *The Tapping Solution*.

This method involves tapping on key points around the head, shoulders and side of one hand whilst reciting words along the lines of *"Even though I have [Name issue or pain], I completely love, accept and forgive myself."* A tapping session typically goes on for about three to five minutes, by spending approximately 20 to 30 seconds at each of the energy points in rotation.

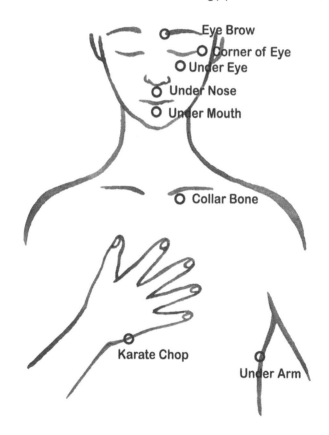

Both techniques build on the knowledge of ancient medicine from China and India, which work with our inner energy channels to stay healthy. In Chinese medicine the meridian lines, which flow through the body, are critical to our health.

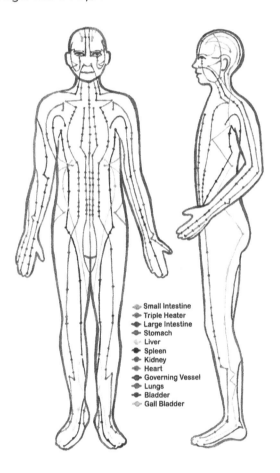

Small Intestine
Triple Heater
Large Intestine
Stomach
Liver
Spleen
Kidney
Heart
Governing Vessel
Lungs
Bladder
Gall Bladder

In modern energy medicine practises, we see elements of the ancient knowledge come into play. For example, the tapping points and healing code areas coincide with the meridian paths or acupuncture points. The statements, which are recited, have echoes of the Sanskrit scripts and types of meditation from Ayurveda, (an ancient Indian holistic health practice), designed to rebalance our mind, body and energy.

These methods are accessible to everyone with little or no financial outlay and are bringing about profound effects in the way people think and feel about themselves.

We can reprogram our mind and unblock trapped energies, through a few simple words and actions. In our modern times, when medicine is tied to complex science and focused on treating symptoms rather than cause, energy medicine offers a compelling and refreshing alternative, which is both gentle and deeply connected, to our relationship with our body and emotions.

I have used both these techniques myself. The Healing Code I found very helpful when addressing recurring symptoms of Irritable Bowel Syndrome (IBS), which had been a growing and increasingly painful condition. I used the Healing Code for about four weeks at daily intervals and sometimes more. The IBS did not disappear immediately, but gradually reduced. What happened as a result of the practice was that I started to listen to my body more, understand the food and emotional choices I was making and key into my body and hear its needs. As a result I started to make significant changes, including eating more wholesome foods, drinking less alcohol and committing to daily yoga practice. I believe that using the code gave me a different level of awareness about my body and its needs, enabling me to make healthier choices to support my healing.

I started applying the Emotional Freedom Technique (EFT) more recently, captured as I was by Nick Ortner's engaging style and the many free online resources he makes available on his website: www.thetappingsolution.com. For me EFT has been particularly effective in dealing with emotions as they arise. As soon as I recognise I am feeling stressed, anxious or imbalanced, I find a quiet space, ideally in front of a mirror to practice EFT, naming the emotion and asking for its release. I find the results for EFT are almost immediate. Within a minute or two of the practice, whatever emotion was present has disappeared or is greatly reduced in intensity.

Call to action

Our emotions are the energetic markers that define our experiences. They give us visceral feedback of a point in time. These emotions can be positive or negative, but none of them are designed to hang around and become blocked in our body or our psyche. They are temporal flashpoints to help anchor our experience. The best way to transcend our emotions is to learn to observe them and create distance between them and our essential self. By building our perspective and learning to appreciate that emotions are only communicating the impact of an event, we can learn to acknowledge it, capture the learning and release the effect. Self-reflection is one of the best ways we can practise this.

Make it happen

There are three exercises to choose from to support your path to emotional freedom. You do not have to do them all. Choose the one that best suits your situation. Remember, it is better to do one thing well, rather than three things badly. Your reflection on the results and your learning will be as important as the activity itself.

1. Keep a journal, noting down your emotional experiences.

   Write down what was happening and how you responded. Write down the nature of the emotion. Give it a colour and a shape. Observe where you felt the emotion in your body and if there were any physical changes you noticed.

2. Develop an affirmation to repeat during times of stress or anxiety.

   For example: "*My emotions will come and go, yet I will remain present.*" Or: "*This situation will pass, all is well.*"

   Whenever you find yourself challenged, repeat a phrase that works for you silently in your mind. Whilst repeating your affirmation, notice your breathing, which will help you stay anchored in the present moment.

3. Practise using Emotional Freedom Technique (EFT) or Tapping.

It is a very simple practice, which can bring about profound changes in your emotional and physical state. The process allows you to tap into and release emotions in a gentle and loving way. The best times to do EFT are in the morning, or at particularly stressful times during the day. One to three minutes of tapping on the points described in this chapter, together with the phrase *"Even though [state the emotion or issue you are experiencing], I completely love, accept and forgive myself."* Practice for one week at least three times a day and journal any changes you notice.

"There is a power, which we all hold, which allows us to move forward with our goals and plans. It is always with us and available to us whenever we need it. That power is Intent."

CHAPTER 4

The Power of Intent

Intention is the driving force in our life. It is the fuel of our actions and gives purpose to our goals. To become intentional and live a life of meaningful action, we need to learn to harness our thoughts and the energy all around us. If you have tried to make changes in your life but find yourself going around in circles or making little progress, learning how to harness your intent will make all the difference.

 In this chapter,
we will explore:

☑ *the nature and power of intent;*

☑ *how to recognise and change our beliefs;*

☑ *how to engage with a compelling vision for our future; and*

☑ *how to set intentions and actions to move forward.*

The focus to succeed

There is a power, which we all hold, which allows us to move forward with our goals and plans. It is always with us and available to us whenever we need it. In fact, it marks out those people who succeed in life through their application of it. That power is intent. To access this power requires only one thing, which is focus, but this can be easier said than done.

During the last 20 years of my consulting career, I have worked in numerous organisations and industries with a diverse range of leaders. Sometimes my work was to turn around the fortunes of a struggling organisation, or to help an already successful company improve further. The difference in the results between these two situations can be very stark and there can be many reasons for this.

The one thing which makes the difference between success and failure is the intensity and consistency of focus applied to the task. Organisations fail when they lack coherent focus, spreading their efforts too thinly and not providing a clear reason for why the changes are needed.

Coming Home to You

Successful companies by contrast, have a laser like focus on their priorities and make a clear link between the efforts needed and the rewards for success.

These same principles can be applied to individuals as well. The difference between success and failure is the power of focus. When a person has a weak focus, and starts many projects in the hope that one of them will prove successful, they are likely to find themselves going around in circles with little forward momentum. When a person has a strong focus, and can link their efforts to their goals and stay committed to their path, they will always succeed, even if they have to experience setbacks along the way. Michael Jordan[7], the most successful Basketball player of all time, said:

"I've missed more than 9,000 shots in my career. I've lost almost 300 games. 26 times, I've been trusted to take the game winning shot and missed. I've failed over and over and over again in my life. And that is why I succeed."

Success has been very much part of my life, but so too has failure. The difference between which one won out was the level of belief I had in myself. Determination and resilience are part of my character and this helped me to focus on the task in hand, believing the effort was worth the reward, despite the hardship or difficulty I was experiencing at the time.

Create the right beliefs

Napoleon Hill[8], author of *Think and Grow Rich* famously said:

> *"What the mind can conceive and believe, it can achieve."*

In the early part of the 20th century, Hill spent over 20 years looking at the patterns and behaviours of wealthy and successful American businessmen (it was always men) to see if he could find the magic ingredient that marked these individuals as special or different. The one thing he came back to, time and time again, was the strength of belief these industry magnates held in themselves and their goals. Each, in different ways was willing to walk his own path, defy the widely-held beliefs of their time of what was possible and take big risks to follow their beliefs.

People who struggle to attain success may be holding self-limiting beliefs of what is possible or what they are capable of achieving. Beliefs are not something we are always conscious of. They can be deeply hidden in our psyche and take some time and attention to find the root cause of. Many of our core beliefs are formed in middle childhood, when we are starting to individuate our sense of self and look at how we compare with others. The messages we receive from people around us such as parents, peers and teachers shape and form our beliefs. We are not always conscious, in our early years, of forming these beliefs about ourselves and the world around us, but they will have a profound impact on how we go forward with our lives for years to come.

One of the earliest beliefs I formed about myself was that I was not a person worthy of success. Based on the messages I received at home, school and from my peers, I continually felt I was second best, or too stupid, poor or clumsy to ever have success in life. For many years, I had this belief hidden away.

On the surface, I was quite a boisterous and strong individual, but deep down I harboured this doubt, which was like a shadow always hanging over my achievements. It meant I left school with no qualifications, went into jobs where I did not have to push myself and wasted many of my early adult years drinking and trying to cover the pain of believing I was not good enough and never would be.

If anyone had asked me, at the time, if I doubted I was good enough, or worthy of success, I would have vehemently denied it, precisely because I did not have the self-awareness to know this was indeed the case.

Dispel self-limiting beliefs

There are many ways such self-limiting beliefs can be broken down and for me the turning point was allowing love into my life. To put myself in a place of being loved and believing myself to be lovable, I was dispelling a long-held belief that I was not lovable, turning on its head an old script, which unbeknown to me had been running in my mind. Believing I was lovable, meant other beliefs, such as 'I'm not good enough' could no longer run; they became incompatible with my new reality. I realised over time that the best way to change a belief is to adopt another one, which is incompatible with it.

To change a belief, we need to understand it and this can take considerable time and effort. The best way we can understand our beliefs is to learn how to question what we are thinking on a regular basis. This will give insight into what has been the anchoring force behind our current situation. By reflecting on the situation, asking questions and writing down the answers, we can understand the patterns that are having a profound effect on our life. Once we have a clearer understanding of our beliefs, we become empowered to change them into new beliefs. And the great news is that changing beliefs can have an instant and profound change on our whole life.

One of the most life changing beliefs I dispelled was my view that I was stupid. Leaving school with no qualifications meant I had a very low opinion of my academic capability. How could I believe otherwise when it had never been tested? When I achieved my first degree in Social Work, I still did not believe it was mine until the day I saw the results printed on the board in my college halls. Up until that moment, it had been beyond my mental construct to be successful in academic study, such was the deeply held belief that I was stupid and would not amount to much. When I saw my name on the list and the result - a 2:1 degree, I was completely shocked. In fact, I just could not take it in. I stood in front of the paper for several moments genuinely confused about what I was reading. To achieve this good result had a profound effect on my misguided core belief that I was stupid. The old belief could no longer co-exist with this new reality. Many of my college peers will remember the elation I expressed in our post-results party, when I kept repeating the grade, which was to convince myself it had been achieved, rather than to boast to other people.

Since then, I have never doubted my academic ability and I have gone on to complete two further Masters degrees and achieved several other professional qualifications.

Belief is like the spark plug in the engine, it will get you started. But it is the vision of what you want to achieve and then the creation of habits to ensure you stay on the journey that will lead to your success.

Build a compelling vision

Belief will take us so far in our journey to success, but it needs to be paired with a clear vision of what it is we are striving to achieve. This is important, because it creates the tension between the current state and what we want, which will drive us forward. This in itself, is a way of breaking through self-limited beliefs, while providing direction and a destination to aim towards.

One of the most powerful exercises I have undertaken was biography work with my good friend and then mentor Mario Van Boeschoten. One of the things he asked me to do was to draw a vision of my life in terms of family, friends, career, goals and to identify what was important to me. He asked me to draw a picture of how I would like it to change in five years' time. Using pictures is a very powerful way of unlocking our thinking and achieving deeper understanding. It is not important what your artistic ability is, but simply to be able to symbolise your needs in a way you can identify with. This allows images and ideas to emerge in a much more uncluttered and free-forming manner, which can rarely be achieved

74

through discussion alone. It comes from a different part of the brain; the more creative and free thinking place, which does not need to follow linear steps to formulate ideas. What was truly amazing about this seemingly simple exercise was that it put in motion an extraordinary set of events. It allowed me to transition seamlessly from a Chief Executive role in a not-for-profit organisation to a management consultant, who would be in the midst of major transformation programs for multinational organisations within two years.

I remember taking those pictures out and reviewing them a few years ago, and I was stunned at how accurately they had described my journey from leader of an organisation to the adviser for leaders of global organisations. It was so specific and precise in all areas of my life. It was like a blueprint that I had unconsciously followed to achieve my goals.

The exercise taught me how important it is to have a sense of the two most important points in our journey; the start; and the end. Change often fails when we only focus on one of those points and not the other. How many times have you seen someone leave a situation because they are unhappy, only to find themselves repeating the same pattern again and again? This happens when we only focus on what we want to run away from, but have less clarity on what we want to move towards. We have created no forward motion to allow us to create a new reality. Equally, we may all know of friends who constantly have big plans, but fail to realise them. Their feet do not seem to be planted on the ground, so they cannot make an accurate assessment of where their starting point is, to help them navigate the journey to achieve their goals.

We can avoid these pitfalls by holding in our mind a clear understanding of what we want to achieve and where we are starting from. Having a powerful vision is a way of focusing our effort and energy on moving towards something new. To move towards this vision, we need to change our actions and the best place to start is with our habits.

New habits, new life

When we have a clear vision of what we want to achieve, we need to look at how we change our behaviours and habits to allow room for the new reality to emerge. Change will not emerge from the heavily trodden path we have already followed. It requires us to lift ourselves from the patterns of our life and create new paths and new space for the real magic of change to emerge.

When we use the word habit, we often see it as something, which is ingrained, historic and imposed on us. Yet habit is merely a series of choices we have made along our journey to help us get to where we want to go. Many of the habits we form are to make our life easier and to stop us having to think about endless choices. They tend to be actions with little conscious energy attached to them and therefore are the easy option. But if we do not review our habits regularly and question whether they are serving our best interests, they can become our prisoners, stopping us from being able to move on and find new ways of expressing ourselves.

The good news is that habits can be very easy to create. We need to focus less on the effort of breaking bad or unhealthy habits and more on creating new ones, which will no longer be compatible with the old ones. This is a much gentler and supportive way to bring about change without using a negative or judgemental inner voice, which is often applied to 'break' bad habits.

Ask yourself what one thing can you start to do for yourself today, which will make a big difference to you and your life? If it is achievable and you can see a definite reward in doing this habit, set your intention to start it straight away.

I am constantly questioning my habits and routines and looking for new ways of doing things. I'm not trying to stop bad habits, but focus on new habits, which will make the old habits less enjoyable and be associated with less reward. Take my writing for example. Yes, these very words you are reading right now. I struggled with myself for years to write this book, having the ideas rolling around in my head. But my habits were all focused on my work, on delivering for my clients, who were demanding more and more from me. And I left my writing until late in the evening and guess what? I had no creative juices left to write anything coherent. One day I started to question some of the underlying assumptions driving this pattern. My beliefs such as – *'I have to deliver to the client first'; 'I'll find the time in-between projects to write the book'; 'it will come when the time is right'.* All of which, led me nowhere, until one day when I simply decided to start a new habit. I decided to start my day at 5.30am and carve out at least an hour every morning to write my first book. This was all it took for me to start a habit, which helped me to overcome one of my biggest barriers, my own thought processes.

Whatever area of your life is asking for your attention, commit to a new habit to support it for three weeks. If it hasn't worked, don't get disheartened or give up; simply try a different habit! Keep going until you find one that works for you and when it does work, stick to it. Over time you will see that crowding out the old habits with the new habits is the best form of change you can make.

 **Call to action**

Living an intentional life is possible to achieve with time and effort. What you need is an understanding of your beliefs, so you can change them and the development of new habits, which will encourage and support your new experiences. There are many ways you can become more intentional and achieve your goals and dreams, several of which are surprisingly easy to access.

 Make it happen

In this section the three exercises are part of a process and you will achieve the most benefit from working through them in order. If you prefer to choose just one, start with the third exercise for creating new habits. Most of all have fun.

1. **Reflect on the beliefs you hold about yourself and the world around you**

   Make a list of the beliefs in three areas:

   - Beliefs about myself
   - Beliefs about my family / loved ones
   - Beliefs about society

   Use these questions to explore your beliefs more deeply and write down your reflections.

   - What is the belief I hold about...(the situation, myself, others...)?
   - Why do I believe that?

- Can there be an opposite but equally valid belief about...(the situation, myself, others...)?
- If I can change my belief - what else can it be?

2. Make a Vision Board

When you have a clearer perspective on your beliefs, focus on developing a stronger, richer vision of how your life will be when you harness your new beliefs. Make a vision board, which includes the following time periods.

- One year
- Five years

For each time frame describe what you want to achieve for your:

- personal relationships;
- professional life;
- home circumstances; and
- emotional life.

The deeper and richer the vision for each time-period, the more of your intent can be invested into achieving it. Use pictures, images, words and whatever other media will help you to emotionally and mentally engage with your vision. When you have completed your vision board, put it somewhere you can see it regularly. Engage with it and add to it, as new ideas emerge. Vision boards are powerful ways to harness our intent and set us on the path to achieving our goals.

3. Create new habits

Habits are also incredibly easy to create, once you have put your intent and vision behind them. It takes three weeks of daily practice for a new habit to form. This means any area of your life where you are struggling right now, can be turned around in three weeks simply by creating a new habit.

- If you don't feel you have quality time with your kids - set a specific amount of time aside, which is dedicated purely to having time with them.
- If you don't feel you have time to meditate - set your alarm 15 minutes earlier in the morning to give it more priority.

- If you want to change your eating habits - set some simple and achievable eating rules you want to test out for the next three weeks.

If your review finds you have not formed the habit, be gentle with yourself and ask what got in the way and what new or revised habit you can try for the next three weeks. Be creative because the options are limitless. Remember each new habit will bring important learning and understanding of what will work best for you.

"If you have ever sat by the ocean and watched its beautiful rhythm of waves, colours and sounds without expecting anything of the ocean or yourself in that moment, you will have touched an inner peace, which is the very essence of consciousness."

CHAPTER 5

The Nature of Consciousness

Consciousness is the true gift of life endowed to humans. It goes beyond our physical form to a deeper awareness of life, its possibilities and our connection to everything around us. Many of us block this consciousness, because of our upbringing, or we become stressed and overwhelmed by life. We can find ourselves living in a constant state of anxiety, unable to let go of thoughts of doom and gloom dominating our waking hours. Yet, when we connect to our consciousness, we can fire up our imagination, create amazing things, build truly spectacular lives and find an unending source of happiness. To do this, we must take the first step, which is acknowledging and welcoming consciousness into our life.

In this chapter, we will explore:

☑ *how to access a deeper state of awareness which is truly transformational;*

☑ *how to become aware of the power of intent in shaping and accessing this awareness to make changes to our life;*

☑ *how consciousness is accessible to us at every moment of our life; and*

☑ *how to find the doorway to our consciousness.*

What is consciousness?

Consciousness at its simplest form is awareness with intent. It is our awareness of the world, universe, energies and the patterns of life around us. Intent is the forward motion of the energy we have to achieve a purpose, based on this awareness. Humans often mistakenly believe consciousness is theirs alone, but it is everywhere and permeates everything. It is in the acorn, which grows into the oak tree. It is in the seed, which grows into the rose bush and the embryo, which grows into the human child. It is in the power of the body, which enables broken bones to knit and scars to heal. It is in the moon's cycle around the earth and the earth's cycle around the sun. There is no aspect of life we can look at which does not contain a level of consciousness.

The more we investigate and deepen our awareness of the nature of consciousness, the greater the mystery becomes of what it is and why it exists. Many people walk through life without thinking deeply about consciousness and they tend to view life as a series of circumstances, which simply happen by some form of happy accident. As my understanding and connection with consciousness grows and matures, I see the most astounding events, which have brought about the amazing diversity of life on this small planet, spinning around a burning star in the middle of an ever-expanding universe. Science is at loggerheads with consciousness and its importance to life, but one pioneer on the subject is the esteemed British scientist, Sir Roger Penrose[9] who offers us a bridge between the two:

"I would say that the universe has a purpose, it's not somehow just there by chance...some people... take the view that the universe is just there and it runs along... and we happen somehow by accident to find ourselves in this thing. But I don't think that's a very fruitful or helpful way of looking at the universe, I think that there is something much deeper about it."

We do not need to have a complete understanding of what consciousness is, to benefit from its presence. Think about gravity, which exists regardless of our appreciation of it. As humans, we have a unique relationship with consciousness precisely because we are able to use the power of our minds to draw on it and shape our understanding of the world through it. The challenge we experience is that the very mechanism, which allows us to do this - our ego mind - also limits our experience of it. Our ego mind, if calm, centred and disciplined, can bring our understanding of consciousness to great heights, but to do this it requires taming.

When we are born, we do not have a quiet and disciplined mind. Our very rate of development means we have this enormous processing machine in our brain attempting to make sense of the world around us by analysing billions of data points per second. In our early months and years on earth, we have little or no discipline to our thinking mind, allowing it to be open to all that is around us. At some point in our development, this mind requires taming and educating.

There are many ways we can tame and discipline the mind but it requires a degree of ownership of our thoughts, reflections and perceptions of the world. When we live as if we are automatons with no influence on the world around us, we have already failed to take the first step towards owning and understanding our very nature.

The key to taming our mind is to open ourselves up to the awareness all around us. By looking beyond oneself and one's own thoughts and seeing the beauty of life, which abounds, we open a doorway to new awareness and thinking.

When we open our awareness, we can learn to separate ourselves from our thoughts, realising we are something distinct from and greater than these random sets of information that are bombarding our waking mind. We can learn to notice our thoughts without becoming attached to them. We can watch them as they rise and fall, much like the breath we take in and out. We can learn to stay in the present moment, actively inviting consciousness into our life. And when we become closer to consciousness we become more peaceful, balanced and centred. If you have ever sat by the ocean and watched the beautiful rhythm of its waves, colours and sounds without expecting anything of the ocean or yourself in that moment, you will have touched an inner peace, which is the very essence of consciousness.

Consciousness knocking

I have spoken already of my early upbringing and the constant state of conflict, distraction and anxiety, which pervaded my childhood. I was a product of my time, no more reflective or aware than any other family member or childhood friend. As I grew older and moved away from my hometown, the habits, patterns and emotions of my past moved with me. I drank alcohol heavily and I ate unhealthily - even as a vegetarian. I created conflict in many of my everyday interactions, seeing small sleights when none were intended or feeling less valued than other people and thinking I needed to prove myself. I lived my life like a victim who had little or no influence on her circumstances.

One thing, which is very obvious to me now, which was not obvious to my 21-year-old self, is that my thoughts will create my reality. I lived in the belief that I was a victim of circumstance, with no say about my life and events conspired to make it so.

One weekend some of my friends from my old life in Birmingham came to stay with me Somerset, where I was working. We had a lovely time together and I remember clearly one Sunday afternoon, we were walking along a beach, the sun shining and our feet in the water, happily chatting. We had a lovely day together and were all feeling very wistful. My friend Pete turned to me and said, "But are you happy Mary?"

I remember at the time not knowing how to answer. "Yes, I suppose I am." I replied. But deep inside me the question started knocking on a door to my inner consciousness. It manifested as this slight niggle with both the question and my answer. During the next few weeks, it came up again and again for me: "But are you happy Mary?" I kept hearing it repeat in my head.

Why such an innocent question came to haunt me, might sound silly, but it became a key turning point in my life. Before that point, I had never truly asked myself if I was happy and if I knew what constituted my happiness. I had never had a notion of whether happiness was part of my life, or even if I had a right to expect it. To some people this may sound incredulous and to others, I rather suspect this simple and profound point might resonate.

When we do not own and appreciate our happiness it cannot be a presence in our life and we miss the constant source of joy it will bring. It is like inviting people around for dinner but then refusing to open the door when they arrive. We are simply not ready to welcome happiness in our life if we do not believe in our right to have it. Happiness is not an emotion, but a state of mind. It is a deep choice, which is connected to our relationship with consciousness. Because we confuse happiness with the satisfaction of consumerism, wealth and power, we think it is conditional and transient, based on certain conditions being met, conditions which are often viewed as scarce and unattainable. We feel we have to strive, work hard and hope happiness will somehow show its elusive form.

This understanding did not suddenly emerge in my young and undisciplined mind, far from it, but what did emerge was an understanding that I can own and pursue my happiness. I had a right to it and I can take actions to move towards it. Within three months of this realisation I had changed jobs, moved to the Cotswolds and was well on my way to finding true love. All because at some level I allowed my deeper consciousness to steer my life and help me make choices. which led to my happiness.

What I learnt through my period of transformation was that my deeper desires and beliefs had a more profound effect on my life's circumstances than my surface thoughts and opinions. Without awakening to my deeper inner world, I doubt I would have successfully transitioned to the next phase of my life, allowing me to take control of my education, career and relationships, which sent me down a new path of fulfilment.

We cannot live without consciousness, but we can live without a true awareness of it. As consciousness is everywhere and part of all life, it must feature greatly in our existence, even if we do not practice the skills to connect with it on a regular basis. My younger self was not particularly reflective, nor contemplative and I missed many opportunities to connect with my inner consciousness. But in some moments I did tune into my intuition and I was guided when it mattered most.

Like an airplane on autopilot, consciousness needs human effort to reach its destination. It needs the engagement of skills, experience and thought to ensure the journey is clear, well-managed and goes smoothly. We achieve the most in terms of our health and well-being when we use the power of consciousness to guide and help us.

Healing and consciousness

One of the areas where consciousness can have a profound effect is with our health and our ability to heal. When we cut our finger, we cannot simply think through the process of healing or tell our finger to heal and watch it happen. Healing is not part of the thinking mind or the ego, but is part of the consciousness, which surrounds us. The finger's healing requires none of the ego mind's effort to heal. It will simply do so through the natural order and code, which exists in its very nature. What has been proven however is our thoughts will directly impact the speed and quality of our healing. Bruce Lipton[10], a pioneer in the field of genetic research and consciousness said:

> *"A person's health isn't generally a reflection of genes, but how their environment is influencing them. Genes are the direct cause of less than 1 per cent of diseases: 99 per cent is how we respond to the world."*

While our genes are hard-coded for harmony with nature and therefore to thrive in a state of equilibrium or health, the environment we place them in, the thoughts and beliefs that surround them will have a greater impact on their overall health than this hard coding. Bruce Lipton through his extensive research confirms consciousness can assist with the healing process. Thinking thoughts of healing, positivity and harmony during times of illness reduces its length, intensity and impact on our body. We therefore have this unique ability as humans to use consciousness to interact with and change the world, to transform it for the better.

This has been well-known for many years and we see it emerge in the Placebo Effect. When modern drug trials test the efficacy of a new treatment, there is always a test group who receive a placebo - a treatment with no active ingredient in it - such as a sugar pill. Sometimes, the control group participants know they are in the placebo group and sometimes they don't. In a significant portion of the placebo group, there is often a reported improvement in their condition, which is measurable, for example, blood pressure, heart rate and brain activity. This has led to research on why a placebo, which should have no discernible impact on a patient's condition, brings about results as good as, if not better than the very drug being tested. The Placebo Effect is an enigma, but we are learning all the time the importance of the connection between mind and body on the healing process. If we believe something will get better (the expectation a pill will work) then it will get better (the result).

Learning to hold positive thoughts, which believe in a good outcome for our physical ailments can be a challenge, but the opposite is also true. If we believe we will suffer and be in pain because of our condition, our belief is highly likely to perpetuate the very symptoms we are trying to relieve. We can fall into a set of beliefs, which tell us we are powerless to interact with the world and we are unable to bring about positive change for ourselves and our circumstances. When we disconnect from our essential nature and from the world around us, everything becomes our enemy, even ourselves.

Our doorway to consciousness

Consciousness is not something we need to go on long journeys to find, or work very hard to achieve, since it is an implicit part of who we are. We come fully equipped with the exact capacities needed to live a fully conscious life. The challenge comes from the world we are born into, which consistently erodes our understanding and awareness of our connection to consciousness. Over millennia, stories have been handed down, telling us that only the gifted few are able to connect with the greater consciousness and the wisdom it bestows. We can see how this has played out in the power structures of our society, in religions, monarchy and political leaders. The impact of these structures is to demote the ordinary person to a subservient role, making us believe we are here to serve the structure rather than our own individual connection with consciousness and our own power and uniqueness.

The challenge is not in finding our consciousness, but in connecting with it on a regular basis. In our activity-driven, technology-fuelled world, we are surrounded by distractions. We have many options calling to us and demanding our attention. Our everyday mind - the ego - thrives on and depends on this kind of distraction as a way to alleviate boredom. Yet even boredom is a sign of our deeper consciousness being starved of its needs.

Once we move beyond the distractions of the outer world, we can find ourselves in a calm and peaceful state. This is why meditation is important for our inner world. Meditation can be in many forms. Walking meditation, colouring meditation, listening to gentle music, or simply sitting and being. The way into a meditative state is always through observing the self and the best way to do this is to focus on the breath.

Daily meditations have the advantage of bringing discipline to the mind and allow your awareness to heighten for longer periods during the day. The daily practice is a way of checking in with your deeper conscious self, providing a much-needed energy and mental boost ahead of whatever the day brings. If we practice in the morning, we can set our intentions for the day, guided as they will be, by our inner consciousness. In the evening, we can use the practice to reflect on our day and see what insights emerge, which can shape our actions in the future.

It is not the process of connecting with consciousness which we can find challenging, but it is more the act of regular practice. Creating time, space and intention to regularly connect with our deeper consciousness can be difficult. Yet we need to consider the flip side of this equation as well. By not doing any regular meditative practice how connected do we feel to our deeper self? Do we meet our goals, or love our self, or feel fulfilled when we fail to connect to our consciousness?

When you feel there is a gaping hole in your life, which is missing something fundamental at its core, investing time to find out what it is will help. You can quietly find time to go into yourself and ask the deeper questions, such as: *Who am I? What is my purpose? How can I fulfil my own needs? How can I contribute to my community?, How can I help others?*

In the previous chapter, I talked about how to follow and fulfil your intent by creating new habits and this might be one of those areas you choose. Start by noticing those quiet moments in your life when new glimpses of reality can be experienced. Find time to become relaxed, calm and reflective. You may not see this as classic meditation, but whenever we allow ourselves to become more inwardly observant and calm, we connect to our deeper consciousness. This is when our creativity emerges; when we can see a different perspective; when we are able to observe our emotional state without having to act on it. When we connect to a deeper reality inside us, it provides a far more reliable rudder from which to steer our everyday life.

 Call to action

Raising our levels of consciousness is more about practice than effort. All of the techniques below will become more powerful over time. The more often you practise connecting with your consciousness, the more powerful the results will become.

You can start by increasing your mindfulness and meditation activities. Start small and notice the difference short practice sessions make. If it feels right, continue. If not, think about adjusting your practice, or the meditation activity until you find one, which suits you. Your consciousness is waiting to connect with you and will bring you on the most amazing life journey when you make the time to become acquainted with it.

 Make it happen

In this section, you have three types of meditation to try. Each one offers a process that in itself will help you relax and connect with your inner life. Do not feel compelled to try them all, since the styles will not suit everyone. Read through and choose the one that feels the most natural to you. The most benefit is achieved from repetition, so ideally commit to the meditation over a three-week period, aiming to have between two to three sessions of your chosen style each week. Reflect on your experiences, ideally writing in your journal, to help you to identify the best one for you.

1. Walking Meditation

If you are a regular walker, build mindfulness into your routine. Ideally use headphones and play gentle music for this activity. Find a gentle classical tune you love. Here is a five-minute routine, which can be repeated, for as long as you need it.

- As you walk, start with a few centring breaths. Breathe in and out for three slow, thoughtful steps.
- Follow this pattern for about 40 seconds and when you fall into a routine, notice the feel of the breath and where you feel it inside your body.
- For the last third of the minute, start to visualise a bright light coming in with each in-breath and notice where it comes in your body. On

your out-breath imagine there is an exchange and you are letting out darker light, blocked energy or tension.

- Now move on to noticing your feet and the movement they are making as they contact the ground. Try to keep your head up and looking forward rather than down at your feet. With each step, slow it down enough to notice, but not so slow you do not feel you are making progress. Notice the heel as it touches the ground, notice the movement of the foot as it rests on the ground and moves towards the toes, notice the last movement of the foot with the ground before it moves off again allowing for the cycle to repeat on the other foot.

- As you are observing the process, you may find other thoughts come to mind, questioning or judging thoughts. If you notice these, simply let them go.

- Imagine an inner smile emerging at the thoughts as we might smile at an indulgent child, with no need to say or do anymore. Follow the feeling and motion of your feet for about two or three minutes.

- For the final minute, move your attention to the breathing in your heart. Notice the breath as it moves in and out of your heart area. Notice the speed of your heart's pattern and whether it feels different from the start of the walk. Notice any emotions or discomfort you feel. If it does feel strained in any way, take a few breaths while visualising a bright white light filling your heart space and breathe out noisily through your mouth with big sighs to release any tension that might be there.
- Continue your walk in this gentle way for as long as you need.

2. Colouring Meditation

You cannot go into a bookstore or newsagents these days without noticing the explosion of colouring books for adults on sale. They have become a new phenomenon in helping many thousands of people become more conscious. If this appeals to you here are some tips on how to use them.

- Buy a book with images and themes that please you. If the images don't make you smile or feel whimsical before you have started colouring them, then they won't after hours of working with them.

- Use a set of good quality pens, but also have the range of colours and shades that you feel drawn to. Buy more than one pack if you know there will be some colours you are always likely to use again.
- When setting aside time for colouring ensure the TV is switched off in the room you are working in and if possible play a favourite gentle music track, a classical tune or meditation music.
- When colouring, notice your breathing. Become aware of your breath going in and coming out.
- When you use your colours, start to breathe the colour into your body through your breath and notice where it seems to resonate in your body. Allow your breaths to become long and hold it in your body for two to three seconds before slowly letting them go.
- When thoughts arise, notice them and give them an imaginary smile and let them go.
- When you have completed your colouring session, take time to notice and admire your work. Thank yourself for making time for you.

3. Guided Meditations

This is closer to the classic, more traditional mediations where we sit upright or cross-legged and enter a calm, relaxed state for a period of time. During these types of meditation, we can leave our daily worries behind and let our body rest while our deeper consciousness takes us on an inner journey. For beginners, it is often easier to use guided scripts to help with this process. You can find several guided scripts on my website, together with recommendations for other resources. Use the tips below to help get started.

- Make a ritual out of these sessions. Ensure you have time on your own with no interruptions. Reduce and background noise and if you have no control of it, wear headphones to listen to your chosen music.
- Gentle aromas can be helpful for relaxing. Consider using an oil burner, incense sticks or scented candles, to create gentle fragrances.
- Relax into your favourite chair, or if you feel comfortable sit on the floor and cross your legs.
- Keep your back straight to stop yourself from slouching.

- Be aware of your head and tell yourself it feels light and is floating above your shoulders. This will help you to align your head over your spine more comfortably.
- Have your guided meditation track playing softly. For your early practices, I suggest you try the 15 minutes Forest Walk Meditation. Or if you have less time, try the five-minute Rise and Shine version. Both are available on my website: www.findyourjoyfullife.com.
- Relax and enjoy the experience. When finished, remember to thank your body for the support it gave you during the process and thank the guided track or music for the benefits you feel.

"Our thoughts are the building blocks of our existence on this earth. When we build strong and positive foundations, our experience is likely to be life-enhancing in every way. When we build crumbling and undermining foundations, life will seem like a terrorising and unpredictable place."

CHAPTER 6

Calm the Inner Critic

The most intimate relationship we have is with our own thoughts. Yet many of us go through life on autopilot, allowing our thoughts to prompt us this way or that, without really questioning their validity or relevance. When you find yourself in a constant state of anxiety or regularly going down negative spirals, where life feels overwhelming or hopeless, a good place to start changing the situation is learning to calm your inner critic.

In this chapter, we will explore:

☑ *how our thoughts shape our life;*

☑ *the impact our thoughts have on our experiences;*

☑ *how to separate our observations from our thoughts; and*

☑ *how to choose and ultimately change our thoughts.*

We are not our thoughts

One of the biggest barriers to achieving positive change in our lives is ourselves. We might look around and point to other people, our parents, colleagues, partners, children, or anything in our circumstances and say; *"This is the reason I cannot change!"* But when we are honest with ourselves, we know these external circumstances are not the reason we cannot change, but only the symptom of a much deeper cause. Most of us go through life without realising we are in control of every aspect of our life and the choices we make. The first and most important of which is the choice we make about our thoughts.

Our upbringing and the society we live in shapes our experiences and our understanding of ourselves. From a young age we are told what to wear, what to say and even how to think.

Our parents shape our existence in early life, chastising our thoughts, reactions and emotions, albeit with the best of intent at heart, but ultimately to ensure our behaviour conforms to societal expectations. We grow up with the illusion that we are our thoughts. Almost as soon as we start talking, our energy goes into pleasing and conforming to the expectations of other people.

This early separation from our inner life is one of the major ways disillusionment settles in and we start to develop a powerful inner critic. This inner critic, which is the constant voice in our mind, grows up with us, becoming stronger over time and by our teenage years we cannot separate it from ourselves. If we have had particularly negative or crushing experiences from a young age, the voice takes on an authoritarian role, constantly keeping us in check. If we give this voice too much space, it starts to take over every waking hour and becomes our master. It tells us what to wear, what to say, how to hold ourselves, who are our friends and who are our enemies. It reduces us to our reactions, forever driven by the changeable world all around us.

When it becomes all encompassing, we end up sleep walking through life, feeling neither one thing nor another. Forever struggling to define who we are and what we want from life. This is a path of struggle, where as adults we find ourselves exhausted, stressed, worn down and we often develop ailments, which show we are not connected to our true selves.

The critic tamed

The path back to healing starts with taming the inner critic. Think about it for a moment. How does your voice talk to you? How much do you allow it to prompt you and send your energies and emotions this way and that?

My own inner critic emerged when I was quite young and one of the biggest influences was my mother, who was a very anxious woman. She was brought up in rural Ireland during the 1930s and 1940s, during a time of depression, poverty and overbearing church influence. Her own self-esteem and inner wisdom had been beaten out of her by her father and by the strict teaching of the Catholic church. Her adult life dealt her further blows causing her to lose all belief in herself and her abilities. When I was a child, my mother was in a constant state of panic and anxiety. She particularly found new experiences difficult and I can remember clearly a day trip we had to Bournemouth, when I was about 10 years old. We had a great time at the beach but on the way back to the coach we became disorientated and the streets started to look the same. Feeling lost and uncertain, my mother started to panic.

If I showed any signs of being too relaxed, or even worse finding the situation funny, she became angry towards me, shouting or hitting me for not helping her to sort out the situation. Yet if a suggestion was offered, her level of anxiety made it impossible for her to hear me. In the end, it took us about an hour to return to the coach, just in time for its departure. What could have been a simple matter to resolve was blown into a major life crisis, which negated any of the good experiences we had enjoyed during the day. My mother's inner critic took over and became an unreasonable monster, punitive towards herself and her young daughter. Over many years this behaviour damaged the relationship between us.

As I grew up, despite my firm belief I would not be like my mother, some of these patterns emerged in my behaviour. If I was in danger of being late for a train or bus, or might miss a deadline, I heard this negative voice, being highly anxious and derogative as I was rushing around trying to address the situation. I heard my voice saying; *"You're so stupid!"*, *"That's typical of you!"*, *"What are you going to tell [whoever I was meeting] now?"*, *"Nobody will trust you again if you arrive/deliver late?"* I was never centred in myself during these times and probably came across as rude and inconsiderate to anyone who was dealing with me, although I believed I was perfectly amicable. During these times of stress, like my mother, I became deaf to suggestions or offers of support from other people because my inner critic was screaming in my head. I fell into the trap of not believing in my own abilities or having faith everything would turn out well in the end, which of course it always did.

It took me a long time to realise these inner thoughts were affecting my outer life. Like most people, I believed they were something that happened and I had little or no control over them. Even when things started crashing around me - computers crashing, technology, transport, I did not make the link that my thoughts and my energy were contributing to my difficulties. Joy, my life partner, has known this for a long time, but I was deaf to her observations during these times of high stress. I was too wrapped up in my own drama to be able to step out of it.

One day, as I was in the process of rebuilding my life after a bad spell of illness and I started to listen and notice my thoughts. I started to see a clearer link between the inner dialogue - which at the time was full of self-pity and helplessness - and my diminishing physical and emotional condition. That spark of awareness was to set me on a new path of getting to know and tame my inner critic.

Observing thoughts

If you can relate to the inner critic, imagine for a moment the voice in your head as a person outside of yourself, as a real physical being, a trusted friend. How long will you feel that this person is your best friend, when he or she starts to turn and sneer at you and call you stupid? How long will you want to hang out with this friend if they constantly tell you that you are not good enough? How friendly will you continue to feel toward someone who is always saying you will have to wait in the wings of life because you will never be smart enough, beautiful enough, or thin enough? I suspect you would have dumped such an imaginary friend pretty quickly because nobody likes this kind of toxic behaviour for long. And yet the voice inside of you, this inner critic is given a lot of room to dictate and undermine your life.

You might be thinking, but it's only thoughts, they don't really have any power. But I say the opposite is true. Our thoughts are the building blocks of our existence on this earth. When we build strong and positive foundations, our experience is likely to be life-enhancing in every way. When we build crumbling and undermining foundations, life will seem like a terrorising and unpredictable place.

Byron Katie[11] a well-known author and the creator of *The Work* a powerful self-help process, which is described more fully at the end of this chapter, suffered for years with depression and self-doubt. One day after a moment of clarity about her thoughts and their destructive nature, she could separate her understanding of herself from the thoughts in her mind. In this moment, everything about her life changed.

"I discovered that when I believed my thoughts, I suffered, but that when I didn't believe them, I didn't suffer and that this is true for every human being.

Freedom is as simple as that. I found
that suffering is optional.
I found a joy within me that has never
disappeared, not for a single moment.
That joy is in everyone, always."

Our thoughts are electrical impulses released from our brain. They do not follow any particular pattern or logic most of the time and can have as much to do with the chemical reactions in our brain as they do with the reality of the world around us. Research using brain scans have revealed that when a thought arises there is a spark from one part of the brain to another. At their most elemental level, thoughts are energy units we create from the energy we breathe in and receive from the world around us.

But where does this electrical spark come from? What fuels the spark? When we connect to a deeper part of our self, where we can slow down our thoughts and observe their birth and journey in our minds, we see them as random thoughts and prompts, some of which are helpful, but most of which are distracting. This observing of the thoughts has two powerful effects. Firstly, we are able to see thoughts without feeling compelled to follow them. We are free to understand the thought is not us and does not have to define our experience. Secondly, the observer of the thoughts comes from a much deeper place of awareness inside us. This observer is always calm, compassionate and loving. The observer does not judge or set conditions for acceptance.

One of the most direct ways of calming the inner critic is to spend time as the observer. Allowing it to watch the thoughts without feeling any compulsion to follow the impetus they create. The voice we recognise as our thoughts is an aspect of our psyche, which has emerged with the ego. It may feel like an inconsequential aspect of yourself, but it has the power to affect not only the quality of your life, but the quality of life for those people around you as well.

Choose your thoughts wisely

Energy has two modes. It can be either positively charged or negatively charged. In electricity, these two modes are essential to make a current of energy flow. In our own bodies, we can build up negative and positive energy. We do this in several ways, but it always starts with our thoughts. Our positive thoughts create positive energy and our negative thoughts create negative energy. One will move us; the other will debilitate us. When you find yourself stressed, worn out and lacking in energy, the first place to look is to your thoughts and what is the quality of dialogue going on in your mind.

Several studies have shown the nature of our thoughts has a direct influence on the environment around us. Those little thoughts and prompts in your head, directly affect you and the world you live in.

The much-debated experiments linking thoughts to the physical world conducted by Masaru Emoto[12], a Japanese writer, appeared to show how the structure of water changed based on the thoughts and emotions expressed around it. He had words placed on a container of water, or words were spoken to the water, or music was played to the water. The water was frozen and the water crystals were photographed. The difference in the quality of the crystals which received positive and beautiful messages, compared to those which receiving negative messages was significant. The water that had been loved and encouraged formed beautiful shapes. The water that had been abused formed misshapen crystals lacking form or symmetry. Although his scientific methods have been called into question, further research by French virologist Luc Montagnier, winner of a Nobel Prize suggest that water does retain some memory of its experiences.

This has profound implications for every aspect of our lives, especially since we ourselves are made up of more than 70 per cent water. You can see how sending negative thoughts to ourselves can have a profound effect on our overall well-being. Another Emoto experiment was The Rice Experiment, which has been replicated in schools across the world. Two identical cooked rice containers were labelled. One marked, *I Love You* and one marked *I Hate You.* Each morning children were asked to repeat the phrases to the respective jars. After only five days a marked difference could be seen in the quality of the rice, with the 'Love' jar remaining white and fluffy and the 'Hate' jar going rancid. The only difference for these jars of rice, were the thoughts being shared with them during the week.

Even if science is not in complete agreement about the way water stores its experiences, the implications could be profound and it points to the need to control our thoughts to control our life. Cultivating positive and loving thoughts will bring positive and loving energy into our life, while harbouring negative thoughts will bring a destructive and stagnant energy.

Calm your inner critic and give it little or no room to influence your world. Make your thoughts sing with praise for the amazing person you are. Let your thoughts show you the amazing wonderful world that abounds all around you. Allow them to take you on wonderful journeys of creativity and innovation. Anytime you feel them taking you down the cold, dark path of self-negativity again, stop them in their tracks and simply smile inside. This one action will be enough to stop the pattern of negativity from gaining any ground.

 **Call to action**

Calming our inner critic requires us to become aware of our thoughts and learn how to ignore the unwanted and harmful ones, while welcoming and encouraging our positive thoughts. To do this, we need to learn to become keen observers of our thoughts, so we can control them, rather than the other way around. This is a skill that can be cultivated with a little time and effort. There are several different ways to control our thoughts and they are surprisingly easy and accessible.

 Make it happen

The three suggestions below can be completed on their own, or together. Choose the one that best suits you and try it for a few weeks. If you need more support, try another activity. There are no hard and fast rules here, since all of the activities will help you become more reflective, which will help to tame your inner critic.

1. Keep a journal

One of the best ways to observe and change your thoughts is to start to write them down. Buy a small notebook, something robust yet light enough to carry around with you and make a note at any time of the day when you notice something. Journal your emotions. Journal what you are grateful for. Journal what you have noticed on the way to work, or during lunch. Journal a conversation and your response to it. Simply start writing and little by little you will see a space emerge between you and your thoughts. The space created is your passport to freedom.

2. Meditate

I know many people struggle with this step, so start small. Set aside five minutes on three mornings a week, where you will be quiet and allow yourself to observe your thoughts. Use an app if it helps, such as Headspace, or one of the many guided meditations on my website, such as The Healing Path and The Gentle Garden, both which are less than 10 minutes. Investing as little as 15 minutes per week on gentle reflection of yourself and your thoughts can make a significant difference to your overall wellbeing.

3. Read and do *The Work* by Byron Katie

If you find you are have a perplexing situation or strong emotions about something, then spending time questioning your own thoughts can be very valuable. Byron Katie has developed *The Work* which poses seemingly simple questions. Take time to ask yourself the following questions and write down your answers honestly. Reflect on the implications of your insights.

1. *Is this thought (about the situation or issue) true?*
2. *Can I absolutely know that it's true? (Yes or No)*
3. *How do I behave when I believe this thought?*
4. *Who would I be without this thought?*

"Health and harmony are achieved through
balance in all areas of our life."

CHAPTER 7

As Without, So Within

When we start noticing and building a more positive inner world, our thoughts and attention will naturally move to our relationship with the outer world. We interact with the outer world throughout our waking hours, at home, school, work and in our personal relationships. The impact we are having not only on our human connections, but on the wider world is far reaching. The choices we make every day, to consume, to take from the world around us, have an impact on the overall sustainability of the earth.

In this chapter, we will explore:

☑ *the link between our bodies and food;*

☑ *how to listen deeply to our bodies;*

☑ *the link between the food we eat and where it has come from; and*

☑ *how to eat mindfully.*

Make peace with your body

Our bodies are physical hosts, which allow our energy to be contained, expressed and to flow. This union allows matter and energy to meet and become an intentional force from which we can achieve amazing things on earth. This energy is often described as the spiritual body. Whilst the energy can exist without the physical body, it is not possible for the body to exist without this essential energy. The physical body works through this spirit and relies on it to function in the way it is intended. The spiritual body is recognised by all ancient traditions. In Eastern traditions, such as Buddhism, it is known as oneness, Hindus call it Atman and in Western traditions, we call it the soul, which comes from the Latin word *Anima,* which means to animate. We know there is an important union that takes place between the energetic body and the physical body when we come into being. When we stay close to this awareness, we live in peaceful harmony with our body. If we do not, it leads to discord and difficulty.

In the West, this separation between body and spirit happens at a young age. We see it in rising obesity, food disorders, increasing use of cosmetic procedures and the lack of connection to our food sources. The body becomes a machine, treated as an object, fed and watered, but with little thought to its healthy maintenance or true nature.

When we consider the body, it tends to be with a critical eye to its external appearance and how this compares unfavourably to other people. Women in particular are prone to this dissatisfaction with their body due to external pressure to conform to unrealistic expectations. Bombarded as we are by images of thin and under-developed models. Our bodies are as diverse as we are. Beauty comes in all shapes and sizes, but always from within. When we start to over-identify with these images we become unhappy with ourselves and start to put our body through harsh regimes to achieve standards it was never designed to meet. The thoughts we send to our body are equally negative and punitive; *"You're fat", "You're thin", "You're ugly", "You're too tall", "You're too short"* or perhaps the most defeating of all, *"You're not good enough".* Since our thoughts create our reality, we are allowing ourselves in these moments to create a battlefield between us and our bodies.

CHAPTER 7: As Without, So Within

When we separate our thoughts from our body, we stop listening to it and its needs. We start to develop body dysmorphia because we are literally unable to see our body the way it is. When someone has become extreme in their eating habits, through too much eating, or starving themselves, they have stopped connecting to their body. The mind and the body are working in two different spheres.

Making peace with our body starts with learning to connect and communicate with it. Our body is a very sophisticated biological organism and can communicate with us in many ways. Pain is a way of telling us something requires attention. Hunger is its way of asking for food. Repeat ailments are its way of drawing attention to an area which needs our help. Our body will prompt us when we need to move, or when we need to stop. It will guide us to specific foods we need when we are lacking something, or guide us away from foods that are unhealthy. Despite this sophisticated communication system, over time our mind has grown stronger and has learnt to ignore it. We can easily override these signals and frequently do, but such denial comes at a cost to us and our health.

Our body as an extension of the earth

Health and harmony are achieved through balance in all areas of our life. Earlier in chapters 5 and 6, we looked at the quality of our emotions, thoughts and internal energy sources. Here, we are looking at how we relate to our body. A good place to start is our relationship with food, what we eat and the impact it is having on ourselves and our planet.

Much of our modern life is about mindless eating, simply satiating a hunger pang and moving on. We give little regard to what we are eating, why we are eating it and where the food has come from. Yet food is one of the most fundamental ways in which we connect with our body. It is part of the constant two-way communication between mind and body, yet it has become distorted and difficult for us to interpret.

Animals in their natural habitat will be governed by the food that is available to them. They will eat what is in season, drink from watering places they know to be safe and learn to fast during harder times such as winter. Animals must work with their body. They have no other choice.

Humans are no different, but we have masked this reality through the apparent abundance of food all around us. With apparently little effort on our side, every possible whim can be met; the winter strawberries; the ready prepared meal; or perhaps the fully roasted chicken for less than a cafe latte at our favourite coffee house.

When we look beyond this mind-boggling choice we see the real cost behind our food abundance. We can see how the convenience of food and the sheer weight of choice enable us to develop unhealthy habits. It has become easy to quieten our body's hunger pangs instantly and continue with our day. Our body and its needs are merely an inconvenience, rather like an insistent toddler trying to break into its parent's conversation, we reluctantly acknowledge it, we pacify it and we move on.

When we stop stifling our body's communication, we can hear what it needs more clearly. Our body will tell us when it needs more protein, or more water or more fruit. The body will rarely ask for sugary or unhealthy foods, since they do not feed any vital organs or biological processes. If we are chasing the quick fix solutions of sugary and fatty snacks, this will be the ego mind, not the body. The ego mind is always thinking about past or future. It will be trying to move beyond the immediate need for food, pushing us on to the next big task. This is especially true at work, which is why stressful times can lead to weight gain. Learning to listen to our body when it is thirsty, hungry, full, or tired is like learning a new language. It can be difficult at first, but over time and with practice it becomes easier.

Over the years, I have sometimes been in tune with my body and listened to it and given it what it needs and at other times I have blocked its cries. When I have not listened to my body I have found myself feeling more lethargic, becoming overweight and lacking any passion or vibrancy not only for my food, but for life in general. When I became stressed at work, I resorted to poor food choices. When I gave myself the space and calmness to really listen to what my body needs, I made much better choices. This dialogue is constant. It is not achieved through one good meal, or one good choice, but through the ongoing interplay between mind and body.

My communication with my body can be strained when I am overworked or tired. I still have habitual triggers for carbohydrates, sugary treats or unhealthy choices, but these are crowded out by more days when food is cherished, celebrated and worked into healthy and nutritious meals.

I do not present myself as the ideal weight or shape, as defined by the external standards imposed on us, but neither do I suffer from the constant ailments and lethargy of the past. As I grow older, I see my body change shape and size, gaining extra bits, where there used to be none, but I notice this with a calm, loving acceptance. I know I will work with my body through these changes and find the best way to address its needs.

When you listen to your body, in the quiet of the morning, or during a stroll in the afternoon, or in the evening before you go to bed, it will give a much clearer message of what it wants and needs. You will start to appreciate the value of eating foods that are at their peak season, rather than those that have been genetically grown. You will also see that not every meal needs to be protein based and your body feels happier, calmer and more energetic without refined sugars or caffeine to prompt it into action beyond its normal limits. Alcohol can be enjoyable at times, but if it is taken to excess, it will create imbalance in our physical and emotional life.

When we question more deeply what our body needs when we are hungry, it will not be the habitual sandwich, burger or sugar filled snack, but a much more varied and nutritionally dense diet. We can question further how was this food produced? What was the impact on the earth in bringing this food to the shelves? When we know in our heart it was neither sustainable nor respectful, will it really be a happy choice for our bodies? Our body breaks down every morsel of food we put in our mouth and all the energy it creates will either sustain us or contribute to our sense of imbalance.

It is not simply a matter of looking at calorific value and fat content in our food and calculating whether the correct amount has been consumed for an ideal body mass index. We must look beyond food as purely nutritional units and become aware of the profound and important relationship it has for us and our bodies. We must learn to make food choices, which are more aligned to the natural rhythm of life.

Our food eco-system

If we take this philosophy even deeper, we start to question how our food is produced. Since the Second World War, the focus across many countries has been on ways to stabilise and increase food production. To cope with this level of demand, science and industry advances have ensured yields on harvest have grown and the cost of production for food has reduced. A typical family can afford and expect to eat meat every day, yet the same family in the early part of the 20th century would have enjoyed meat less than once a week.

In post-war industrialised nations, the illusion that we are doing well because we can afford to eat meat and dairy products, hides a much greater truth and a bigger threat to our health and the health of the planet than perhaps any other human activity.

If the cost of sustaining the growing human population is unsustainable to the earth, we all have a responsibility in changing the system we now find ourselves enmeshed in. With the rise of modern farming and extracting techniques, we believe we can take ever more from the earth with little or no harmful consequences. But the cost in the long term is incalculable. We see more of the earth's surface becoming desolate, our oceans becoming polluted and the increasing habitat loss for other species as they compete with humans for food. A recent study by The World-Wide Fund for Nature[13] found the global population of all vertebrate species has dropped by 50 per cent in the last 50 years. While data from the World Bank[14] shows the human population has more than doubled to nearly eight billion in the same period. The only species growing in numbers alongside humans are those that are used for food production, such as chickens, cows and pigs. WWF reports:

"This loss of wildlife is startling, and people are at risk, too. Without action, the Earth will become much less hospitable for all of us. We must consider our impact on nature as we make development, economic, business, and lifestyle choices. A shared understanding of the link between humanity and nature is essential to making profound changes that will allow all life to thrive for generations to come."

CHAPTER 7: As Without, So Within

We want food to sustain and develop us, but we cannot separate this from the integrity of how the food was produced and modern farming practices. These include:

- grain and soy, which is heavily modified or has cleared natural habitats of other species for its production;
- fruit, which is forced to ripen out of season; and
- vegetables, which are heavily sprayed with pesticides.

Such farming practises undermine the nutritional goodness we can normally gain from eating these foods. Yet nowhere is the direct relationship of what we eat and how it is produced more deeply troubling than in the area of meat production.

By treating animals as mere commodities, we forget that like ourselves they are energy beings in an energy universe. Our modern production methods have created cheap meat, but there is nothing painless about the process from the animal's perspective. Pigs are held in pens, cows live their entire lives in stalls with no access to pasture land

and chickens live in overcrowded sheds with barely enough room to stand.

Fast forward to the typical weekly shop at the supermarket, where we are presented with plump chickens at a great price with a '100 per cent natural' promise, or pork sausages which are 'Farm Fresh', complete with comforting images of animals in bucolic scenes of happiness, far removed from their reality. It's easy to see how our curiosity or concerns are easily assuaged. When these items are consumed, they cannot help but have some of the energy of the animal and its journey to our table within it, along with all the stress, suffering and pain which may have occurred along the way.

The arguments to justify intensive farming methods are based on food production levels and demand. The human population is predicted to grow by a further third by 2050 and will require a 70 per cent increase in food production[15]. This often-quoted statement suggests if we keep doing what we are doing with even more intensity we will be able to meet this demand. But it belies a much bigger issue, which is the so called efficient methods of modern farming, which are in fact much less efficient. According to Compassion in World Farming[16]:

"For every 100 food calories of edible crops fed to livestock, we get back just 30 calories in the form of meat and dairy; a 70 per cent loss.

In short, people are being forced to compete with farm animals for food."

Solving world hunger, reducing our devastating impact on this planet and becoming more humane in our relationship with other species is possible, but involves us making different choices in what we consume and how it is produced. Without bringing our relationship with the wider eco-system back into balance, we cannot hope to find a place of balance and harmony in our own bodies. We are inextricably linked with the environment around us and the consequences of our choices.

We are what we eat

In the last 50 years alone Western diets have become dominated by meat and dairy products and yet our diet during thousands of years has included cereals, grains, berries, vegetables with occasional meat and dairy. We are forcing animals to make huge jumps in their growth rates, yield and body mass to meet our demand. We can produce crops that have a greater yield, broiler chickens three times the size of their predecessors and get cows producing more dairy than pre-war times. Research from Advocacy for Animals[17] found that this increase was staggering:

"Between 1950 and 2000, the number of dairy cows in the United States fell by more than half, yet during that same period, the average annual milk yield more than tripled."

What this does to the cows being forced to produce milk beyond their natural capabilities we can only imagine, but it does not paint a picture of a harmonious life. We cannot deny the overall health of the human population since the Second World War has increased dramatically, including dwindling infant mortality and average life spans increasing by 40 per cent worldwide[18]. Whilst mortality is on the decrease, its more stubborn cousin morbidity is on the increase. Protein and sugar rich diets of the post-war era are taking their toll on our health as the global statistics for obesity, diabetes and heart disease reflect. Our path to health involves us making more mindful food choices, which support our planet while improving our wellbeing.

 **Call to action**

It is not too late for us to learn to walk lightly on this planet, consume less and build a greater respect for all species, which share it with us. We are part of a finely balanced system of life, one which has taken millions of years to create. Our own bodies are a microcosm of the larger ecosystem that supports it. To reach a point of peak health and vibrancy in ourselves, we need to make choices that align to the peak health and vibrancy of our planet.

How we consume in the world has a direct impact on our overall health, as well as our planet's. Learning to build a lighter, more delicate relationship with the world around us is part of our path to healing, one is dependent on the other. While all consumption should be mindful, it is our relationship with food that is perhaps the most pivotal in our journey to a more balanced relationship with the earth.

 Make it happen

The following suggestions are very much mix and match. You do not need to work through them in any order. Start with whatever activity feels right for you and explore the others at your leisure.

1. Eat mindfully

Be fully present while eating your food. Make time to sit down at a table. Take a few moments to think about the food you are about to eat and give some thought and thanks to where it came from, how it was produced and what it will bring to your body in terms of nutrition. Enjoy every bite and if you find your mind starting to wonder, or if you are looking at your watch, stop, smile and return to appreciating your food. If you are in the habit of eating at your work desk, start to eat in the canteen. In the long run, it is better for your body and for your productivity. It gives your digestive system the proper time to appreciate the food it will digest and allows you to gain perspective between you and your work deadlines. Do it for one week and see the difference in how you feel about your food and your work.

2. Read the labels of your food

Look at where food has come from and what is included in the ingredients. If you are seeing items that you don't understand or cannot interpret, question if you want to put them in your body.

3. Question more deeply your motives and needs for food

Before buying an item, ask yourself; *Do I really need this? How will I use this? Will I enjoy eating it?* If you are buying something out of habit, especially if it is an item you find yourself throwing away at the end of the week, ask yourself if there is something more interesting and enjoyable to take its place?

4. Educate yourself on the food industry and its impact on the earth

We make better choices when we understand where food has come from and how it was produced. The reason intensive farming and

Genetically Modified, GMO, has risen so dramatically is because there is very little accountability. As many of us are unaware of how our food is produced, it has allowed producers to make decisions on our behalf, which are not always in our best interests, but serve their interests for profit and growth. Research the foods you eat and how they are produced. This will help you to make more informed choices for yourself, your body and the wider world, which we all need, to sustain it and ourselves.

"By mastering our relationship with time, we master our relationship with ourselves. We can learn to live in the present moment and through this, connect to a deep inner peace, where stress and troubles disappear."

CHAPTER 8

Timeless Living

In our modern times, many of us are enslaved by time, believing we will never have enough. We are in a constant state of anxiety that there is too little time available for us to fulfil our goals or meet our self-imposed deadlines. By believing time is something external to us, a factor for which we have no control, we are disempowering ourselves and watching our life spin out of control. Yet scientists agree time is not linear, it does not travel in a straight line, nor is it the same for everyone. Our own experiences of time are in fact extremely elastic, as seen by the timeless moments we can spend gazing at an ocean, or the sense of a blink of an eye, when our attention is diverted by something engaging and pleasurable.

There is a place beyond time in which our soul dwells, which is not measured by seconds, minutes and hours. To find our peace, purpose and home, we need to see beyond the illusion of time, to a place where we are free to live the life we truly want. We can learn to become the masters of our own time, by changing our relationship to it.

In this chapter, we will explore:

☑ *the origins of time;*

☑ *what ancient civilisations can tell us about time;*

☑ *how to live in the present moment; and*

☑ *how to live timelessly.*

Living by numbers

Modern urban living has become obsessed with time. We wear our own timepieces or use our smartphones to check the time every minute of every day. We want to measure every aspect of our living. How much we weigh; how quickly we can run, walk, cycle; how quickly we can travel; and how quickly we can cook. Everything in life has become a numerical target by which we place a value on ourselves.

Living by numbers is a key contributor to the Western epidemic of stress and stress-related illness. We have lost contact with our essential nature and instead we have started to live according to whatever set of arbitrary values we place on ourselves. Eckhart Tolle[19] in *The Power of Now*:

*"Why does the mind habitually
deny or resist the Now?
Because it cannot function and remain in
control without time, which is past and future,
so it perceives the timeless Now as threatening.
Time and mind are in fact inseparable."*

By saying time and mind are inseparable Eckhart Tolle is reminding us how our everyday minds, the ego minds are wedded to time. But what is time and does it matter to us anyway?

Time, as we believe we experience it, travels in a straight line starting somewhere in the distant past with a number of events marked along it and somehow it arrives at the here and now, this very moment.

This perception holds us in a place where we believe ourselves to be a product of our past and our circumstances. When we project into an uncertain future, we place conditions on life to conform to a set of criteria that our ego mind creates and is usually not wedded to our reality. The illusion and the myth often tumble down around us, because we find the world unwilling to conform to our view and deep dissatisfaction can settle in.

Much of the cause of our everyday strife and stress can be tracked back to our relationship with time. How we feel about our job, our relationships, our age and our status, will often have roots in how we are viewing time. We may hold deeply rooted beliefs that we do not have enough of it, or it is slipping through our fingers at an unsustainable rate making us feel less effective and therefore less worthy than those around us.

The origins of time

Originally the oldest time measurements were of lunar cycles, until the ancient Egyptians began to measure solar cycles, which became the standard for calculating modern calendars. Time in older civilisations was used to mark important events and to allow for stories to be handed down from generation to generation. This allowed ancient wisdom to be passed on from one generation to the next, helping to safeguard their peoples' future knowledge. Time was respected as a marker to help understand the greater arc of the earth's journey of which we are all a part.

At some point, the shift in our focus of time moved from the general to the specific. Instead of it being focused on understanding the greater wisdom and journeys of our ancestors it became about us, it became individual. As soon as we burdened ourselves with individual time, we created stress, anxiety and suffering. My time became different from your time. My importance became different from your importance. My value became different to your value. This separation led to the birth of the ego as a power centre in our mind, separating us from life. It became our master and we, the essential self, became the slave.

As we know now, far from being linear, time moves in cycles. The earth moves around the sun in 30 days and the moon around the earth in 28 days. Solstices and equinoxes happen at precise points in the year. But no one cycle is the same as the other. They do not mark a plot in a timeline, but merely a cycle.

All of life has an ebb and a flow. A time for growth and a time for recession. We see this in the seasons, in the growth of plants and trees, and in human life as well. While we experience an overarching arc of life in birth, growth, maturity and death, even this does not move in a straight line. Hence the cells taken from two octogenarians can show a different level of energy and activity, based on many factors including lifestyle, environment and genes.

Trees are traditionally aged by the rings of their bark, yet no two rings are the same. Some are thick, some are thin and many appear to merge into one another, hiding their story deep within themselves. They do not experience life as a straight line, but as a series of present moments spreading over hundreds and sometimes thousands of years.

One of the oldest stone symbols in existence points to the ancient people's understanding of this cycle. In Newgrange in Ireland, there is a passage tunnel that is more than 5,000 years old. It is certainly older than the Egyptian pyramids at Gisa. Not only does this extraordinary site pinpoint accurately the exact moment when the Winter Solstice happens each year, it also has a symbol, which points to timeless living, the Triskele.

Part of the Entrance Stone markings, Newgrange, Co. Meath, Ireland

The Triskele is three interlocking spirals at the entrance of Newgrange, which given the craftsmanship employed in carving them and their prominent placement at the site, suggests they were of vital importance to the ancient race who built this monument.

The cycles are all interlocking which conveys the interconnected nature of all life. The celebrations of the winter solstice at this site, were a recognition that the darkest day had dawned, but it would be followed by brighter days.

This huge monument must have taken many generations to complete at a time, when to our understanding, scientific and building materials were rudimentary. Yet, here stands something with unerring accuracy that can light up a passage with a central stone deep in its structure at the precise moment when the winter solstice dawns. Why such extraordinary efforts were invested in creating this edifice is lost in the annals of time. But it does tell us of the deep reverence the ancients held for time, not as a straight line but as a life-giving cycle.

We are often taught through history lessons and museum exhibitions of early human life, of lives of limited resources, hunters and gathers who were mostly nomadic or resided in small communities.

But does this over-simplify the existence of people who could create structures over several generations of such complexity, that even with all our modern advancements we would struggle to replicate? Does this point to a simple and isolated life? It rather alludes to a puzzle, to which we hold only a small amount of the pieces.

If we hold the view that modern beings are at the pinnacle of knowledge and sophistication, built on the toils and tribulations of our more primitive ancestors, it tends to blind us to other possibilities. We block out the signs and symbols that point to educated, well-organised and highly-technical societies. Signs including: the Ancient Egyptian's Pyramids; the Greek's Acropolis; the Mayan's cities and temples; and the Celt's henges and passage tombs. Many of the most ancient archaeological sites known to us have used technology that remains beyond our comprehension.

The arc of life

We simply do not know, based on our limited view of how they once lived, how these ancient civilisations managed to build such edifices to these exact specifications.

What we get a glimpse of, with the benefit of hindsight, is the reverence by which life was held, precisely because there was an understanding of its fragility. All of life has an arc, things will be born, grow, decline and die. Therefore, there was an implicit understanding that all points in life were precious and to be celebrated. We see when civilisations moved beyond this reverence, building on their own arrogance of their superiority, that even this had its own arc of life.

We know about the rise and fall of the Roman Empire, Babylonians, Egyptians and the Mayans. But there could be many more civilisations with complex and sophisticated knowledge and technology at the heart of their society whom we have simply not discovered yet. The Triskele symbol of Newgrange, suggests life moves through integrated and interlocking cycles, constantly moving through ebb and flow.

How can we use this thinking to our advantage? How can we bring timeless living into our busy, time-bound lives? Part of the answer lies in a shift in our mindset. In *The Power of Now* Tolle reminds us the only moment when we are truly alive is in the present one.

The past no longer exists and the future can only be guesswork, where our ego has projected ideas and thoughts of many possible outcomes. By calming our ego mind and connecting with the present moment, we can free ourselves from many of our everyday stresses and worries.

Live for the moment

When we can live more in the present moment, we can pay attention to time as a very small proportion of our thoughts and feelings. Time has a place for all of us, to help us schedule, plan and ensure we catch the train or plane and arrive at the right destination at the allotted time. But this is as a periphery activity. It is not, nor should it be, the deciding or driving factor of our thoughts and feelings.

For example, in my life, time became a dictator, when my career grew and my advisory roles became more senior and influential. When my working life became more driven by targets, deadlines and deliverables, time became a constant companion in my thoughts. The irony of the situation was the more obsessed I became with time and my perceived lack of it, the worst my timekeeping became. I was constantly late for appointments and deadlines as I spiralled into thoughts of lack and scarcity. My world became smaller as I became obsessed with what the clock said, rather than being able to look at the big picture.

My stress levels increased intensely and it was one of the contributing factors to my eventual health breakdown. I had to stop running on the treadmill I had created or I was going to wear myself out. When I took myself off the treadmill and started to look at what life meant to me, I was able to readjust my relationship with time. As my consciousness of the here and now grew, my enslavement to time decreased. I started to see a world of opportunities open up, as soon as I stopped feeling something else was in control of my life. The time monster was tamed and my own inner time machine began to emerge.

Time has become one of the dictators of our mind and is one of the key points of stress in our life. As we rush around from one appointment to the next, it has nudged us into feeling there is never enough time and whatever our actions, we will never catch up with ourselves. We start to believe we will always be chasing our tail to make up the time we have wasted or lost. An inner dialogue of lack or anger will emerge, constantly bickering at us about why we are not good enough or achieving as much as other people. We reach the end of our days exhausted, collapsing into our beds for a restless sleep, only to wake up feeling lacklustre and with a sense of dread about the day ahead. We are not living our lives; our time monster is.

We can stop this treadmill and step off, as soon as we realise our conscious mind not only surpasses time but has the ability to create it for us. Not by giving us more than 24 hours in a day, but by giving us an awareness of every moment within each day. When we allow ourselves to step out of the linear, defined view of time, which our modern living has encased us in, we can see the potential for living in the current timeless moment. Buddhism teaches that the only time is now. The present moment is the only one in which we are alive. The past and future are purely illusionary, having no basis in reality because we are always looking at them through a lens of the here and now, the only moment which exists.

Once we start to become the masters of our own mind and allow time to become subservient to us, we start to lift the burden of stress immediately.

When we learn to stay focused on the here and now, with a deeper connection to our breath, our inner life and our real intentions, a lifetime of timeless living awaits us.

 Call to action

The most critical aspect of time that we can learn to master is our conscious awareness of it. Through this, we can speed time up, we can slow it down, or we can travel to a place of complete timelessness. By mastering our relationship with time, we master our relationship with ourselves. We can learn to live in the present moment and through this, connect to a deep inner peace, where stress and troubles disappear.

 Make it happen

There are many activities you can do to help you live more timelessly and below are several you can mix and match to suit your lifestyle. The more you relax and enjoy the time you spend with these or any activities, the more you can connect to your timeless inner self. Do not feel constrained by the list below, be creative and follow your heart and it will always lead you to a timeless place.

1. Observe your thoughts

Notice points in the day where you start to feel stressed and anxious and observe the thoughts behind these emotions. See if there is a pattern around your time and not having enough of it that is emerging. Journal one or two instances every day for a week to see what beliefs you may hold and the patterns they are creating in your life.

2. Leave your watch at home

Try this for a day or two during the week, ideally on work days. If you catch yourself looking for your watch, ask yourself silently in that moment, what is it about time I need to know right now? What thoughts are prompting me to believe time is important right now?

3. Create relaxation time simply for you

Find a day when you can carve out an hour or two for yourself. Don't let anything impose on your enjoyment of this time. If your mind imposes a time-bound thought, simply notice it, smile and carry on with your activity. At the end of your day, journal how the session felt and what shifts you observed inside yourself as you noticed your thoughts about time arise but did not become distracted by them.

4. Sit and wonder at something timeless

Take the time to sit by an ancient tree or by the ocean, or in the mountains. Allow yourself to relax and simply be. As you connect with your breath and feel yourself letting go of your everyday stresses, start to appreciate the timelessness of your surroundings. Notice the sense of how your own time pails when placed against the greater magnificence of the natural world. Harness the sense of the present moment as you connect with this reality and remind yourself of the wholeness of your connection with time, as you appreciate it through the eyes of nature. Journal your experience and reflections. If you enjoy it, repeat!

"Coming home to you is about reconnecting the three important aspects of our life: our body; our mind; and our spirit. Our energy, thoughts and physical body are designed to work in harmony to bring us to a place of wholeness."

CHAPTER 9

Coming Home To You

In modern times, we have become disconnected from our body. We fail to link our actions and thoughts with our health and wellbeing. Our body holds its own intelligence, through a complex web of energy centres and deep cellular intelligence. It has the ability to harmonise and heal itself. The reason we do not observe this phenomenon all the time is because we have forgotten: how to communicate with our body; how to honour its subtle energies and cleanse and clear it when it has been exposed to a toxic environment for too long.

In this chapter, we will explore:

☑ *the destructive patterns we create to mask pain and fear;*

☑ *how to unblock trapped energies using simple techniques;*

☑ *the energy centres of the body and their role in our healing; and*

☑ *how to meditate to improve health and wellbeing.*

My journey home

During my wild days of drinking and partying, I had no idea of who I was or what I wanted from life. I was like tumbleweed, being thrown this way and that without a clue as to where I wanted to be. It felt like someone or something else was in control of me and I was helplessly watching as life unfolded around me. My young adult days were filled with alcohol, parties, dating and hangovers. There was little of that period of my life that I can look back on with any sense of happiness. Much of it passed in a blur of addictive, repetitive, destructive behaviours.

I resorted to binge drinking to help me relax in social situations. However, I was unable to distinguish between relaxing and reaching the point where I was losing myself in a boozy blur. I had little sense or reason to judge the difference between the two.

During this time, I believed I was demonstrating my independence and proving my worth. I was working, had left home and I did what I wanted, when I wanted, with whomever I pleased. But I was deeply unhappy and lacking in self-worth. I drowned my confusion and pain in alcohol in the belief it helped.

If my more mature self could have come along and had a chat with my younger self at an opportune time, perhaps much of my painful learning could have been avoided. But life is never simple and all of us have our own journey to travel with all the challenges that brings.

My life partner and the love of my life helped me to see that drowning myself in alcohol on a regular basis was not the most productive use of my life. Slowly, I learned the importance of living life rather than letting it pass me by. I learned how to take myself and other people more seriously.

This became the start, rather than the end, of my journey back to me. I had become so disassociated with myself I hardly understood my inner life and emotions. I found it hard to process any negative emotions, such as anger, fear and sadness because they had been repressed for most of my childhood. Many people describe the point of their emotional unravelling as the point when they started to feel safest - when they had found someone they loved and could depend on - and I was no different. The long-buried emotions I had carried with me for many years, started to surface in the early years of my relationship and at times seriously challenged us.

The three keys

Three things helped me through this transition from wild child to settled adult. The first was choosing to return to education and studying for a degree. Up until this point, I had never thought of myself as studious or intelligent, having left school with nothing to show for it. When I returned to education and started to thrive on the challenge of learning, it was clear this was a passion of mine. I started to appreciate my curious mind, my thirst for knowledge and I recognised my ability to solve complex challenges and build coherent theoretical arguments.

Once I realised I had a good brain and a wish to use it, it opened many doors for learning and growth. Even now I am the eternal student, always reading and looking for the next challenge. We have limitless capacity to learn and adapt and by opening our mind to the world around us, we can truly be empowered. We are no longer held by the limited concepts, experiences or doctrines of our childhood. Knowledge when pursued openly really does set us free.

My second big passion, which emerged through my working life, is for people and their development. I have a natural curiosity for and genuine compassion for people. I love how they think, how they feel, their dreams, hopes and flaws. A consistent thread from my younger days was this burning desire to help other people. Once I aligned my career to this passion it took off. It no longer felt like going from job to job, chasing the next set of promises or the next pay rise. It was as if I was in a groove, a path specially made for me. It simply felt right.

The influence of my Autistic sister Bernie and my appreciation of her needs, as well as the challenges of growing up in a chaotic, dysfunctional family made me a good fit for Social Work.

When I felt I had gone as far as I was able in this chosen field I allowed my core passion to guide my next move. When I moved into management consulting I specialised in people and organisational development.

The third area that helped me enormously was my spiritual awakening and the practice of meditation. Many people who have taken a more enlightened path speak of a single moment of clarity when they ask the deeper questions about the true nature of life. Michael Singer[20] in *The Surrender Experiment* describes how this happened for him. He was at home watching sport on television with his brother-in-law when he became aware of this incessant voice in his head always prompting him to do 'stuff'. It was his separation from the voice and the realisation there is a much quieter and calmer observer behind the voice that helped him on his path to awakening. After he had opened himself up to the possibility of something greater and wiser than his ego voice, dramatic changes started to occur. His life opened to an extraordinary set of events, which led to considerable economic and spiritual success.

For me there was no such blinding moment of realisation. After a period of working in Angola I became very ill. At first it was a form of dysentery, but on returning home, there was a systemic breakdown in my immune system causing bout after bout of illness. After many visits to the doctor with little improvement, I started to think there must be another way. I felt I was being viewed as a collection of symptoms rather than a whole person, with each treatment working in isolation to the other drugs that had been prescribed. It was my natural curiosity and my tendency to challenge the status quo, which helped me to think of possibilities beyond those being offered by traditional medicine. I realised I was playing the role of the sick person and accepting the fate handed to me, rather than finding another solution.

I sought a second opinion from a registered doctor in private practice who was also an alternative healer. What took place in Dr Millie Saha's consultation in June 2009 was both extraordinary and ordinary in equal measure. After taking down my medical history she started to work, not on symptoms, but on energy. She worked on my chakras - the energy centres of the body - and within a short time found the two areas, which were blocking my healing. She found I had blockages in my heart chakra affecting my ability to love and be loved.

I also had a heavy and stagnant energy in my base chakra, which is the energy centre governing our sense of security. This explained my need for control and why I believed things would fall apart without my involvement.

In less than one hour she accurately pinpointed my issues. On leaving her consulting room I felt altered. I was light-headed and knew something important had taken place, but was unable to say exactly what. This introduction to energy medicine was to change the way I thought about the body, thoughts and the healing process. Dr Millie Saha[21] has documented her approach in her book *The Twelve Principles of Light,* which discusses the chakras in detail.

My road to health was by no means straightforward or quick after the visit, it took at least another 12 months of hard work and belief to achieve, but eventually I was free of every ailment that had dogged me. It was during this period of recovery I started to meditate. It came naturally as a sort of nudge deep inside me. It was not something I had tried before and had up until that point been a very unlikely candidate. Through my daily practice, I stopped being super busy, rushing from one assignment to the next, driven by targets and deliverables. Instead of believing there was never enough time to do anything, I saw I had plenty of time and unlimited choice in how I spent it. I started to understand how the power of my mind, my intention and my thoughts shaped my life and my happiness. Meditation helped to bring space and balance into my life, two of the key ingredients required for healing.

Unlock your energy

In earlier chapters I have discussed the importance of our energy in affecting our thoughts, body and health. Ancient Chinese and Indian traditions identified the energy systems flowing in the human body. The body is made up of energy which can either flow or be blocked depending on our lifestyle, thoughts and beliefs. We have thousands of meridian lines across the body and it has already been medically proven that these energy centres contribute to our health and wellbeing. The well-known practice of Acupuncture - the insertion of needles into meridian lines - is now endorsed by the UK government as an accepted treatment for some ailments. The meridian lines meet at seven major energy points in the body, called chakra centres each of which have a different function for health.

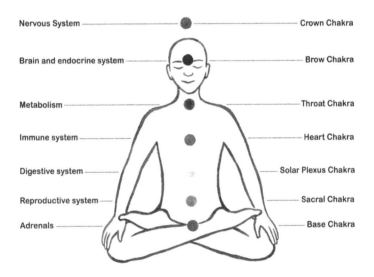

Nervous System	Crown Chakra
Brain and endocrine system	Brow Chakra
Metabolism	Throat Chakra
Immune system	Heart Chakra
Digestive system	Solar Plexus Chakra
Reproductive system	Sacral Chakra
Adrenals	Base Chakra

- The **Base** Chakra, associated with the colour **red** creates security, connection to the earth and sexual health.
- The **Sacral** Chakra, an **orange** colour is linked to creativity, nurturing and new ideas as well as digestive health.
- The **Solar Plexus,** a bright **yellow** sun acts as the core energy for our entire system and is associated with grounding, sense of belonging, personal power and focus.
- The **Heart** chakra, typically represented as **green**, is where we develop our feelings of love, compassion and connection to others.
- The **Throat** Chakra, a **blue** colour, is about expression, clarity, truth and authenticity. It supports written and spoken expression.
- The **Brow** Chakra, also called the third eye, is associated with deep **indigo** and is the centre for intuitive thought and deep knowledge.
- The **Crown** Chakra, which sits above the head is associated with the colour **white** and is the opening of our energy system to the wider energy source, a point of renewal and cleansing for the entire body.

We can bring balance and healing to our body by spending time on each of the chakras in turn, contemplating its qualities and the areas of the body it supports, to bring about a feeling of balance and refreshed energy. The chakra colours can be helpful for visualisation, as well as a way of understanding a need in your body, which you cannot quite put your finger on. For example, if you find a colour dominating your choices it might be the corresponding chakra system is communicating a need. The colour orange might point to a block in creativity or the colour blue to an issue with communication. A simple meditation focusing on the colour will help uncover your need and how best to respond to it. An exercise for this is included at the end of this chapter.

We need balance across all the chakras to achieve optimum health. If there is one centre which is blocked or over or under developed it will cause problems for us somewhere in our physical, energetic or emotional body. Harmony is achieved by developing all the chakras together and allowing for regular maintenance of the energy centres to maintain balance.

Other forms of meditation for healing and harmony

Other activities help with chakra balancing include Yoga, which is one of the oldest traditions working with the energy centres. It is very beneficial in bringing about alignment across all the chakras. There are many different schools of Yoga and some are more challenging than others. If you are a beginner, the Hatha or Iyengar Yoga may work best for you. If you prefer more intensive sports, Ashtanga or Bikram Yoga might suit you more. As little as two classes a week can make a big difference to your overall wellbeing.

Meditation has often been called the inner healer because of the extraordinary results that can be achieved. Many scientific studies have shown how it can rewire the brain, greatly reduce stress and help to bring about physiological changes to assist with healing. There are many different forms of meditation. It is important to open your mind to the many ways it can be practised to find one that suits you best. Often, we see images of the eastern tradition of Zen meditation, which is typically a seated position, legs crossed and eyes closed. This works for some people, but not for everyone. There are many ways we can practice meditation, some of which may genuinely surprise you. You can meditate while you count your breaths, while you gaze at the moon, while you walk, while you eat and even while you pursue an activity, which draws you into a restful state, such as painting or colouring. Meditation is the simple act of letting the mind relax, connecting with your breath and observing your thoughts.

Through meditation we start to become aware of and maintain the energy balances in our body. It is one of the simplest and most complex practises we can do in life. It is simple because it is merely about connecting to our breath and observing our thoughts. Complex because our everyday mind, the ego mind, is an incessant jumble of noise and impulses constantly trying to keep us on the move. The practice of meditation allows the space to emerge from the ego mind and the deeper self, the one that is always calm and connected to the greater source of wisdom. This is what it is like to return home to yourself. To develop a sense of self which is deeply rooted in an understanding of life, the universe and our place in it. When we are deeply rooted in this way, we develop a confidence and a faith in life, which is unshakable.

 Call to action

In returning home to ourselves, we learn to make peace with our body, to treasure the freedom it brings us and work with it to bring peace and harmony to our lives. Coming home to you is about reconnecting the three important aspects of your life: your body; your mind; and your spirit. Our energy, thoughts and physical body are designed to work in harmony to bring us to a place of wholeness. When this balance is lacking in your life, spending time practising the unblocking of your energy power centres will prove beneficial.

 Make it happen

Exercise one below is a full meditation session I have written with the express purpose of helping to unblock your energy centres. Try it from the script below.

1. Practise Chakra Meditation

The process involves using your breath to bring attention to different energy centres in the body. Take a few centring breaths to relax the body and quieten the mind. For each chakra take three breaths. A simple process to follow includes:

- Start with the first chakra – **Base**: bring your attention to the area between your hips and breathe into it. As you breathe in, visualise the colour red and repeat silently, *"I am anchored to the earth"* and as you breathe out, silently repeat *"I release all that no longer serves"*.

- Moving to the second chakra – **Sacral**: bring your attention to the area below your belly button - about three fingers width down and breathe into it. As you breathe in, visualise the colour orange and repeat silently, *"I nurture my talents and create my own destiny"*. As you breathe out, repeat silently *"I release all that no longer serves"*.

- On the third chakra - **Solar Plexus**: bring your attention to the area above your belly button - about three fingers width up and breathe into it. Visualise the colour yellow and repeat silently, *"I centre and focus my energy"* on the in-breath and *"I release all that no longer serves"* on the out-breath.

- On the fourth chakra – **Heart**: bring your attention to your heart. Visualise the colour green and repeat silently, *"I allow love to flow through my heart for myself and other people"* on the in-breath and *"I release all that no longer serves"* on the out-breath.

- Moving further up, we come to the fifth chakra – **Throat**: bring your attention to this area and breathe into it. Visualise the colour blue and repeat silently, *"I express my truth and authenticity"* on the in-breath and *"I release all that no longer serves"* on the out-breath.

- At the sixth chakra -**Brow/Third Eye**: bring your attention to the area between your eyes and breathe into it. Visualise the colour indigo and repeat silently, *"I connect to the wisdom in all things"* on the in-breath and *"I release all that no longer serves"* on the out-breath.

- For the last chakra – **Crown**: bring your attention to the crown of your head and breathe into it. Visualise a bright white light and repeat silently, *"I have an unbroken connection to the* *universe"* on the in-breath and *"I release all that no longer serves"* on the out-breath.

If you are an audio learner, you will find a downloadable guided meditation on my website: www.Findyourjoyfullife.com

2. Join a local Yoga class

Ideally, a gentle form such as Hatha Yoga. Build up a regular practice of Yoga moves.

3. Do daily body check-ins

At the beginning of each day, as you stand in front of your mirror, before you start your daily routines, take a few centring breaths and ask your body; *"How do I feel today? What areas need particular support or attention today? How can I best support my body today?"* After each question allow yourself two or three breaths and let your mind go quiet. Notice if any ideas or pictures emerge, or whether you have any physical feedback from your body. Acknowledge any messages and say thank you. Finish your mirror work by saying *"Thank you for all you will do for me this day."*

"Building courage allows us to break out of the confines our fears place on us, widening our horizons. It enables us to build bridges with other people and contribute positively to humanity."

CHAPTER 10

Courageous Living

Courage is often a quality we see in other people but rarely in ourselves. We look at heroic acts and view them as belonging to more capable people, while forgetting that the small gestures we make can be equally courageous. Courage is how we learn about our character, values and purpose. By stepping beyond our fears and taking actions towards our goals we find our inner courage. Courage emboldens us to stay on the path of fulfilment. We need to live courageously so we can flourish and grow.

In this chapter, we will explore:

☑ *the nature of courage;*

☑ *what is everyday courage;*

☑ *how courage transforms us and other people; and*

☑ *how to recognise and harness our courage.*

What is courage?

When we hear about courage, we often think of heroic pursuits in the act of major conflicts, such as war. We associate courage with individuals who have achieved something exceptional, brave or out of the ordinary in the face of danger. We idealise these individuals and call them heroes and set them apart from ourselves. We see courage as some unusual quality, which only a few possess and we must look on and watch from a distance, in awe.

Courage is indeed these things, but it is far more. It is not something that is only given to a chosen few, but rather it is inherent in all of us.

One dictionary definition of courage is *"the quality of mind or spirit that enables a person to face difficulty, danger, pain, etc., without fear"* (Dictionary. com). Another definition is, *"to do something that frightens one"* (Oxford Online Dictionary). I think the reality is found somewhere between the two. Courage is when we are faced with a danger or a challenge, feel the fear of having to overcome it and do it anyway. When we face challenges in life, no matter how big or small, there is generally a test facing us, to help us to understand our strength and our abilities. If we do not face our difficulties, we never know the true depth of our being and what we are capable of. To go through life without such tests, would be to live a half-life, a life that has brought little in the sense of happiness and achievement.

Courage is like the tempering of steel in the forge. The best swords are always those that are fired repeatedly to become the best version possible. Life is our forge and it will fire us repetitively so we can become the best version of ourselves.

Opportunity knocks

I can think of several times in my life when I have been tested in this way and I had to find a deeper response. When I was at school I was once singled out by the class bully. She was a fearsome and aggressive girl and many of us were frightened by her. When she singled me out for a fight, I did not feel courageous, I felt scared. Even now, decades later, I can remember the exact moment she turned on me and the rising fear I felt. But there was also something else, a deeper resolve somewhere inside me. I knew I had to show up for the fight, even if the odds of success were hopeless. I had to show up not simply to save face in front of my peers, but to show up for myself. I could not allow myself to be silenced and cowered, merely because someone else felt the need to subjugate me.

I somehow knew this was a situation, which would arise again if I failed to address it now. The fear would return in different ways until I had mastered it. This resolve brought some deep inner strength, which I was too young to appreciate at the time. This girl saw something in me, which made her think twice about taking me on. Even though I had no clue how to defend myself and whether I could cope with the pain of her onslaught, my overriding thought was to stand my ground. We had a full audience of classmates around us and yet suddenly, she was not prepared to take the chance of having to fight hard to get the upper hand. She sucked in her breath, threw her chin at me and said, "Nah, you're not worth it" and walked away.

I was baffled at the time and many other bystanders were confused by what happened. In that moment, I learnt an important lesson in standing up for myself no matter what the overwhelming odds of failure may be. Not only did it help me build my self-respect, it also gained the quiet admiration of my peer group. It lent to me an over inflated reputation that I was able to look after myself and allowed me to see out the rest of my school days without incident, for which I was grateful.

Our character is a sea of potential inside us, waiting to emerge and show us what is possible and how freely and fully we can live our life. To do this, we must listen and respond to the tests that are thrown our way. When we are asked to show up for our self, to meet our strength, understand our value, we have choices. We can hear the call, or we can ignore it and let it pass by. Sometimes the call is to build strength and belief in our self, but other times it is about building our sense of responsibility to other people. I was given exactly this sort of test on an ordinary day on the London Underground.

Many years ago, whilst taking the tube, a loud group joined our carriage. Their voices carried across the carriage and had a menacing air about them. Like most commuters, I had my head down in a book and was lost in my own world, trying to ignore their boisterousness.

As the journey progressed, the crowd thinned and the group started to become more threatening and territorial. Their behaviour took a darker turn when they focused on a young man sitting alone at the end of the carriage. They swarmed around him and the dominant member of the group was goading the other three. As I watched this situation unfold I realised it needed defusing fast or it could quickly escalate out of control. I looked around and saw that nobody else in the carriage was about to act. This was my call to action. I could either decide to ignore it and quietly wait for my stop, or I could see it for the injustice it was and do something. These are pivotal moments in our journey and they do of course come with risks. But life is full of dangers, we face them every day when we leave our homes and sometimes inside our home as well. The danger is not the real point of the situation, it is our response to it and our ability to put our faith in a larger, wiser intelligence that will guide us through.

I put away my book, introduced myself to the dominant member of the group and engaged him in conversation about life in general, asking questions and showing an interest in his life. This disarmed him and his group. To feel warmth, acceptance and genuine interest from a stranger was completely unexpected. As our conversation unfolded, he became animated and expressive. His friends calmed down and lost interest in the young man.

Michael, their ringleader turned out to be a pleasant, if lost young man. He shared his hopes and dreams with me and described his struggles in finding work and somewhere to live. I left him with my business card and an offer of help and possibly a job, but I never heard from him again.

When I intervened on the tube that day, it was not from some heroic urge. When I engaged Michael in a conversation, I knew it had to be genuine and authentic in every way, or else it was not going to work. I saw him as my equal, worthy of my respect, even if I did not respect his behaviour. The conversation that played out between us was completely unplanned and had no specific purpose beyond distracting him and yet it ended up being transformative. I saw him stop, become reflective and then genuinely engage with me as he shared his difficulties, thoughts and ideas. I facilitated his thinking in a kind and supportive way, allowing him to see himself as someone with potential, rather than a disenfranchised member of society. The whole conversation lasted perhaps only ten minutes, but when he left the carriage, he and his group had become calm and friendly. A little bit of courage on my part helped to turn a threatening situation into a cause for hope.

The transformative power of courage

Like me, I guess there are many such times in your life when you had to step up and become involved. These moments point the way to our true journey and soul's purpose. We all have this amazing transformative power inside of us, simply waiting to express itself as life throws up these challenges. We can view these moments as opportunities, or we can see them as threats and build walls to protect ourselves against them.

Courage is an essential ingredient in the recipe for life. We need to be willing to step into our own light and allow the potential of it to unfold in front of us and guide our path. Courage allows us to live our life on our terms and not get drawn in to the expectations and restrictions other people want to place on us. It empowers us to live a full and happy life.

Courage does not need to be idealised, or seen as the qualities of a few, but reclaimed for each of us. Courage is not about the glorification of war and violence, or the superhuman acts done during times of crisis. It is in the simple, every day activities we all do to honour ourselves and serve society. It is in owning our simple transforming abilities to show a better world, a kinder, more compassionate and more loving world to ourselves and those around us.

The Cellist of Sarajevo[22], is a novel based on the true story of a classical cellist, Vedran Smailović. He lived in Sarajevo during the time of one of the longest sieges in modern warfare, lasting nearly four years between 1992 and 1996. Nearly 14,000 people were killed and many more injured by the shell bombardment and sniper attacks from the Serbian forces surrounding them. The citizens of the city lived a furtive hidden life, moving carefully, under constant fear of being shot or killed, while they scavenged for food and water. Smailović fought back with the only weapon at his disposal, his love of music. Every day he came out of his apartment and played classical music in the midst of the gunfire and shell attacks. He brought hope to a hopeless situation and people started to gather and listen to his beautiful music. For a brief moment every day, people were lifted out of the horror of their situation and transported to a place of beauty, potential and hope. They were transformed by the simple act of someone sharing the most vulnerable and beautiful part of their heart and soul, despite the horrendous situation happening all around them. This is the true nature of courage.

Even if you do not see yourself as courageous, I believe you are more courageous than you know. It only takes one step in the right direction to set you on your true path. It might be as simple as saying no to someone who bullies you into doing something you dislike, or spending time with someone who is facing a terminal illness, or sharing an opinion at work which is at odds with the majority. A moment, a choice, an intervention, no matter how simple, can bring you closer to your true nature.

 Call to action

Courage can transform you into someone who is more sure, supportive and beautiful. It's like a muscle, which simply needs exercising to activate it. You can find many opportunities to test it out, to temper it on the fire of life, so you can become the most courageous version of yourself.

In this chapter, we have explored the nature of courage and how we can integrate it into our everyday living.

Building courage allows us to break out of the confines our fears place on us, widening our horizons. It enables us to build bridges with other people and contribute positively to humanity. If fear is a limiting factor in your life, it is time to develop your courage muscle.

 Make it happen

The following are ways to build your awareness of your already courageous actions. The first exercise is looking to your past. The second to your current situation. The final exercise is about your future. Working through them in turn will help you to appreciate the reserves of courage you can already call on to help you to make changes in your life.

1. Reflect on the courage you have already shown
   Look back on your life and at times when you had to stand up for yourself, someone else, or for a set of ideals. Remember what it was which drove you to take action and how you felt before, during and after the action. Write down your reflections in your journal.

2. Be courageous now

Think of one area of your life right now where you believe you can be more courageous. How can you change this situation and transform it into something better? Make a note of your reflections and write down the benefits that being courageous will bring to your life and other peoples. Draw up an action plan with timelines to help you commit to the new behaviour. If it feels like a big step to complete on your own, draw on the support of a friend who is positive and courageous. Let them know what you are intending to do and ask for their help in completing your goals.

3. Build your future courageous self

Draw up a personal manifesto of what you stand for, how you will show up for yourself and other people and what you will be prepared to do if you see unacceptable or unworthy behaviour in other people. Make the language as clear and simple as possible, so it feels like an everyday conversation with yourself. When you feel it is exactly right, print it out and put it somewhere you will see every day.

"Once we lighten our relationship with money, we are free to observe the emotional reactions we have around it. We can learn to become gentle and welcoming towards money and loosen our emotional attachment to it. This allows us to become more generous, kind and willing to let money flow without feeling we are losing something of ourselves in the process."

CHAPTER 11

Find Value Beyond Money

Money is an important aspect of modern living. We can do very little without it. Yet our relationship with money has become skewered over the years. It has gone from being a method to value the exchange of goods, to being a way of valuing ourselves. This has caused us to become disconnected from our true worth, believing it is valued by external factors such as money, or what can be bought with it. This is extremely degrading to our self-worth and leaves us feeling we can only be of value to other people, based on the external worth we display. We can however, regain a healthy relationship with money when we start to separate our sense of self from the money in our life.

In this chapter, we will explore:

☑ *the money paradox;*

☑ *the origins of money;*

☑ *money and our psyche;*

☑ *how to separate our sense of worth from money; and*

☑ *how to understand and change our beliefs about money.*

The money paradox

What separates us from every other species on this planet is the unique invention we created several thousand years ago, to bring about simplicity and freedom to the movement of people and trade. Creating an object designed to represent a unit of value was the birth of money. It became the concept that defined us as human above all other inventions. This one thing defines our existence on earth as distinct from every other creature. Money however, was to come at a cost. One so high it may threaten not only our existence, but the earth itself. The paradox of money is thus: the thing that has marked us out as human, has also created the conditions for us to become de-humanised. We have learnt to place value on this inanimate object to the point where we no longer value ourselves. In this chapter, we will look at the history of how money came about, how it affects our daily lives and what we can do to transcend the money trap.

The birth of money

There came a point in early human history, when we had reached the limits of what we could achieve in our bartering system of exchange. As travel across land and sea became possible and explorers started to travel great distances, early humans were exposed to new food, textiles, tools and minerals, which would be highly prized for their rarity in their own lands. A dilemma arose about how to possess these great items, when early explorers had little to exchange in return. To overcome this dilemma, promissory symbols were created, initially in the form of natural stones and later becoming minted coins. The promise was to receive an equivalent value in goods to those that were being exchanged at the time. This was a simple and brilliant solution to the problem.

The practice of using a symbolic value to enable trade dates back at least 10,000 years. Archaeological finds suggest early currency was a mixture of items, including minerals, livestock and grain. The difference between those early trading civilisations and our experience of money today, is how the value has moved beyond goods and services and into the arena of valuing humans. We are no longer equal, but ranked according to the wealth we have accumulated.

The last taboo

In modern times, we cannot conceive living without money. It pervades every thought and all the choices we make. Money has become more than a value of goods and services, it has become a way of measuring human life as well. We must bargain and haggle to justify the money we receive for our toils.

Nothing can incite strong feelings of resentment and entitlement quite like money. We see it in the everyday interactions all around us; the hotheaded response when someone is overcharged; the resentment at work if someone viewed as less talented is promoted; or when we do not receive something for which we felt entitled. We lose our rationale the moment we identify with this sense of loss, when we perceive something as intrinsically belonging to us is being taken away. It is not the loss of money, but the loss of our own equilibrium, which is corrosive to our society. We have lost our own sense of value in our pursuit for the value we are attributing to money.

Despite the overwhelming need for money, which is expressed everywhere, it is still one of the most unlikely conversations to bring up in polite company. It is as unthinkable to ask someone about their salary, as it is to ask them about their sex life. Money may be a personal obsession, but publicly we must give the illusion that all is well.

It feels as vulnerable to discuss our finances with friends as it is to walk down the road naked. We are judged, categorised and treated according to the material wealth we can display. Our worth comes down to our bank balance. Rather than face feelings of worthlessness, we avoid talking openly about the money we earn.

The money trap

Money is neither good nor bad, but the value and beliefs we ascribe to it can be. From the early days, when money was purely functional to allow for trade between groups, it grew into a complex web of transactions across the world. Money started to become an item to be amassed and displayed, bringing power, control and domination. Approximately 10,000 years ago, when humans shift from a nomadic existence, toward agriculture-economies, we start to see big differences in the power and influence between nations. The spending power of one dynasty could dwarf another, creating conflicts which frequently fuelled war. From around 5,000 years ago, when big dynasties, such as the Egyptians, Babylonians and Mayans are evident, money became political. National wealth became a way of gaining power over neighbouring states.

Gross Domestic Product (GDP) was introduced as a measure for our modern economies just after the second world war. We all contribute to the growth of our nation's wealth, which is measured by the amount of products and services we produce as a nation. The more we produce, the higher our ranking in the GDP stakes. We have created one of the greatest illusions of our time; money will set you free! If we work harder, grow more, increase trade, all will be well! Yet this illusion of never-ending growth is killing us and killing our planet. In Chapter 7: As Without, so Within, we looked at the impact of the unyielding demands that we are making on this earth to produce more food. We are slowly eroding the earth's natural sustainable systems in our quest for more growth, more choice and greater wealth. We created the roller coaster of capitalism, a white-knuckle ride from which we may never be able to get off.

Yet, when the great capitalist machine fails, we do not blame the system, instead we become depressed, resentful and for some even suicidal. We are unable to see beyond the illusion of the money trap, instead taking it as a symptom of our own failure, rather than a failure of the system we have created.

We must remind ourselves; money by itself has no value. It is only symbolic of the value we place on it. Tying our sense of worth to money is like sailing on a boat with no motor, sail or rudder. It is at the behest of the winds and the oceans. It might ride some fantastically high waves, but equally might run aground on a low tide.

The way money fluctuates on domestic and international markets is a lot like the boat lost at sea. It has no stability and is in a constant state of flux. By tying our value to such a mercurial resource, we will find our own sense of worth fluctuating and lacking any sense of depth and consistency. Thus, we live in a constant state of fear and anxiety of never having enough; not being able to earn enough; and being judged by other people for not being good enough. None of this bodes well for a peaceful and calm existence. We need to revisit the basic beliefs we hold about money and how these control our emotions and thoughts.

Money and our psyche

Money encourages us to externalise our value, relegating our inherit worth to a number. The view that we are somehow more whole, worthy or acceptable, based on what we own or can afford creates deep divisions in society. It also fuels unsustainable growth in the quest to have more and more to justify our inflated status.

The gaping hole, which we feel in our own worthiness, can be filled we are told, by buying our way out of it. If you buy this dress, those shoes, that sports car, the designer watch, all will be well. Consumerism is fuelled by our sense of inadequacy. Everywhere you look, there are adverts showing happier, thinner, more desirable people selling us goods, which will make us the same. We believe we can buy ourselves into self-worth.

I can remember feeling like this when I was living in a bedsit when I was 18 years old. I was relieved I had left my childhood home and the shame I felt about it, but I was lost in my newfound freedom. I felt worthless and lonely and to mask my feelings of adequacy, I was caught in a cycle of debt and repayment because I drank too much and purchased things I didn't need, nor could afford. On the outside, I was confident, independent and able to do what I liked. Inside, I was driven by fears of not fitting into society, not being good enough and the gnawing ache of my growing debt. I kept a little red book in which I recorded everything I earned and spent. If the book did not balance I became anxious and scared, not knowing where the money was coming from next. Yet I could not break the habitual impulse buys or binge drinking. I was driven by a desperate need to fill the hole inside of me. I did not consume based on need, but on want, only what I wanted so desperately was not for sale. My self-worth would never come off a hanger or be found at the bottom of a glass and yet it took me many years to realise this. I believed everyone around me was whole and happy and only I felt this pit of emptiness inside. I compared myself to other people and believed, if they appeared more successful, more wealthy, they must be a better person, a worthier person than me. I believed wealthy people were happier and more secure in themselves.

In later years, when I was to work with wealthy individuals, I saw that the opposite was true. They had bought into the illusion that money sets you free, but somehow still felt insecure and uncertain. There comes a tipping point, when money goes beyond being a ticket to freedom and becomes another prison. People of considerable wealth can equally have fears and anxieties about money that are based on how much they have amassed; how much it has grown; or whether the stock market has been kind. They may check their stock values daily and hourly sometimes or boast of their property, their possessions or the expensive schools for their children, believing this is the way they will gain respect from other people. Money becomes a part of their every waking thought, as it does for someone at the other end of the financial spectrum. Both are driven by a fear of being good enough. For the wealthy too, there can be a pit of emptiness at the core of their being.

Our money beliefs

What we think and feel about money shapes our experience with it. If we believe that 'money is the root of all evil' we will unconsciously shun money and abundance. If we believe money only belongs to a selected few, we will find little money coming our way. If we believe we live in an abundant world where money will flow where it is needed, our experience will follow accordingly. As discussed in Chapter 4: The Power of Intent, our beliefs shape our existence, since they have an energy that attracts energy at a similar wave and resonance.

Most of the time we are unaware of the feelings we hold about money and the signals we are transmitting. We don't notice the tightening of our chest while paying a bill, or the rising anger when we have paid too much for an item. These emotions simply appear and with them an energy that transmits our money beliefs to the world. To understand our beliefs, we need to become keen observers. By observing our thoughts and noticing our emotions we create space to raise questions about what may be driving our reaction and find ways to change our beliefs.

I had to break through a belief I was holding about my worth and my salary expectations, when I applied for a promotion at work. The job paid 30 per cent more than my current position. I held the qualifications and the ability to do the job, but still believed I was not worth the salary. It felt too big a jump for me to expect to earn the same money as the incumbent.

I believed I was not worth the rate for the job and I needed to be grateful for what I was given. I believed my worth was determined by other people and I had no right to assert it for myself. In fact, sadly I believed that to assert my expectations was 'unladylike' and showed a lack of gratitude for what I had.

Many people hold this belief, especially in the workplace, when the negotiation for a pay rise can be such an angst-ridden conversation. Women particularly struggle with naming a price for their skills and often don't expect the market rate. It is a sad fact, after years of campaigning for gender equality and social reform, women still earn on average 20 per cent less than men for the same role and skills[23].

I needed serious coaching to breakthrough my limiting beliefs and my partner Joy helped to prepare me by role-playing how I was going to answer the question, "What are your salary expectations for this role?" We didn't stop until I was confident enough to ask for the market rate without waffle, justification, squirming or avoiding eye contact. It took about one hour and 20 repeats of the question for me to get the force behind my words to make it sound as if I believed I was worth the salary being asked. It paid off and I secured the role and the salary. This taught me an important lesson about valuing myself and it shattered my negative beliefs about money and my worth.

Since then, I have become dispassionate during negotiations involving money which has brought about many upsides. I find I can negotiate my commercial rates, discounts on purchases and broker deals easily. I no longer assign emotions to the money or to the outcome of the conversations because I see and believe in the abundance around me. I also believe that if this deal or negotiation does not come off, something else will. I can now allow a natural flow to occur in my conversations about money and stay open-minded and positive. Money has not set me free, but my renewed beliefs in my own worth has.

Regain a healthy relationship with money

We cannot suddenly decide we no longer want or need money, since it is very difficult to survive without it. It is an essential part of our daily living. When we are struggling to pay our bills and keep a roof over our heads, money will be uppermost in our every waking thought. When we have an abundance of money, but a mindset of scarcity, it can equally dominate our thoughts. Both mindsets leave us in a state of imbalance. We are constantly oscillating between the past and the future, remembering past financial troubles or fearing future woes, while allowing the present moment to slip by unnoticed. We need to stop our mind racing during our financial turmoil and learn to connect with a deeper inner wisdom. Without this presence of mind, we are unable to access the thinking that might alleviate our source of suffering. We cannot be creative or reach insights to guide our actions because we are too busy feeding our suffering instead.

What can change our relationship to money however, is relegating it to an auxiliary role in our life. We can choose to see money as merely another factor in our life, such as food, drink and possessions. It comes and it goes, but we are always the constant, we are always present.

As an inanimate object, money has no appropriate way of measuring our worth. It only brings a means by which we can make choices in our life. By separating who we are from the money we have, we can take the emotions out of any transactions. When we are free of our emotions or hidden beliefs, we can view our situation more objectively. We are then free to make better choices about our work, our spending and our priorities.

Benjamin Franklin[24] reputedly said:

"Money has never made man happy, nor will it, there is nothing in its nature to produce happiness. The more of it one has the more one wants."

By loosening our relationship to money and making it something that is part of our journey rather than the destination, changes start to occur. We start to feel more comfortable letting it flow in and out of our life. Money becomes transient, rather like the air we breathe. We cannot hold on to a breath because there comes a point when the body needs to let it go. By letting go of one breath we are ready to welcome in a fresh new breath of air. Money can be experienced like this. We are not trying to hold tightly on to every bit of money that comes our way, but learn to release it to allow more to come.

Once we lighten our relationship with money, we are free to observe the emotional reactions we have around it. We can learn to become gentle and welcoming towards money and loosen our emotional attachment to it. This allows us to become more generous, kind and willing to let money to flow without feeling we are losing something of ourselves in the process.

From this gentle place, we can start to have conversations about money, which are themselves light, clear and unemotional. We see value not only in ourselves, but in everyone. We can be respectful of the needs of other people, while still stating what we want. Discussions around salary no longer feel like an emotional minefield, but a clear and rationale negotiation. Agreeing the price on a big purchase feels playful and builds rapport with the other person, leading to an amicable agreement. Money becomes a neutral component in human interactions based on respect, understanding and compassion.

When we get to this point, we free ourselves up to enjoy life without the constant burden of worry and the incessant thoughts about having enough. We can transcend the illusion of money, no longer believing money sets us free, because we know our freedom comes from within. Money is no longer the object of our life, simply a means by which we can be of service to other people. We start to view the world not in terms of monetary value, but in terms of human experiences and how to best contribute to the greater whole. We are able to connect to our deeper life's purpose, because our line of sight is now set on a more distant horizon.

 Call to action

Money will not set us free, but when we stop imprisoning ourselves with money illusions, we become dispassionate and calm around money matters. Our self-worth is not found in a bank note or earthly goods, but in our actions. We can improve our relationship with money by exploring the underlying assumptions and beliefs we hold and by learning to change these to healthier beliefs.

 Make it happen

For your practical exercise, there is a single process for you to complete over a couple of days. It will help you to identify the underlying beliefs you hold about money. By taking time in-between steps three and four, you allow your deeper sub-conscious to work, which will bring deeper and richer insights as you build your new set of money beliefs.

1. Make two headings on a page. On the left write, *'The best thing about money is...'* On the right write, *'The worst thing about money is...'* Now without thinking too hard about it, write down all of your thoughts and reactions to each list. Do it quickly - no more than 10 minutes in total for this exercise.

2. Take a break for a short while and come back to the list afresh. Circle all the comments that ring true for you. Try to achieve an even number across each column if you can. Ideally two to three comments in each column.

3. On a new page, take each of your circled comments in turn and write it down as a phrase in full, at the top of a page: The best thing about money is [insert your phrase]. Then ask yourself these questions: *"Why do I believe this thought? When did I first become aware of it as a belief,*

which I held? Where would I be if I let go of this thought"? Do this for each one in turn.

4. Sleep on your thoughts. Never do anything further in the same day. Come back to your list the following day or later the same week and after reading through your notes, start a new page and answer this question: What are the beliefs I want to hold about money? Write down the statements that come to mind. Make them positive and observe your thoughts and your energy while you are writing.

5. Finally, take 10 - 15 minutes to connect to your new beliefs. Sit quietly and follow your breath as you relax. Sit and observe your thoughts, allowing them to come and go like butterflies as your mind starts to calm and become quiet. Allow a sense of space to emerge as you settle in to your breathing and relaxation. Start to repeat your new beliefs to yourself silently, two or three times. Then allow silence to follow. Smile and enjoy the rest of the day. Repeat your money mindfulness session once a week for four weeks to deeply embed your new beliefs.

"Work does not define us, but our thoughts
around it do. We can find meaningful work
through the meaning we place in it."

CHAPTER 12

Meaningful Work

Our jobs are such a big part of our lives and when we are not happy at work, it can colour every aspect of our lives. Work defines a large part of our lif e, precisely because we spend so much of our time there. Yet, when we look around, we find many people are dissatisfied with their work; feeling trapped and unable to see beyond their current circumstances; held down by fear of losing money; status or support for their family. Work is necessary for our financial health, but also for our mental and emotional wellbeing. It is one of the ways we can contribute and find our place in society. Finding meaningful work in which we can be true to ourselves and see the value we bring to other people is the way to a fulfilling life. Perhaps the work you are doing right now can be meaningful, with a change of perspective, or you may need to think of moving on to a more challenging role, which better suits your skills and talents. Exploring your relationship with work will allow you to see the possibilities that abound all around you.

 **In this chapter, we will explore how to:**

☑ *find meaning at work;*

☑ *connect to a deeper life purpose, even in challenging work environments;*

☑ *bring your unique talents to the workplace; and*

☑ *find the perfect match between your talents and the work you do.*

Working life

How we work and where we work defines some of the most significant relationships in our life, beyond those with our family and friends. It shapes our existence in a way that few other activities in our life do. We need to work to meet the essentials in life such as a roof over our head, food on the table, warmth and security. How we approach the world of work will often define how we approach life in general. We all come to this life with a purpose that may not be entirely clear to us as we make our way along our path. Many people believe meaning comes from what we do, not what we think. Our work can be one of the key anchors in our search for meaning.

How we work, rather than what we do will define the quality of our experience. We can find meaningful work as a librarian; a fireman; a refuse collector; or as a doctor. The meaning is not inherent in the work, but in the importance we place in it and the level of heart-felt connection we bring to our everyday activities.

Our lives are filled with hours of employment, yet the level of fulfilment in those hours seems to be dwindling. During times of economic uncertainty, such as our current times, people can feel more trapped in a job they dislike. According to recent research by the Chartered Institute of Personnel and Development (CIPD)[25], less than one in two people are satisfied at work and more than a quarter of employees are looking for alternative employment. This paints a very unhappy picture about our overall employment experience.

Many of us are thrust into the world of work with little thought of what we want to do and what is important to us. We assume our meaning comes from what we do: how much we are paid; how we are assessed, measured; and valued by our employers; and how our work status is viewed by those around us. The perceived value of us as human beings is so hard-baked into our work, it will often be the first thing someone is asked when meeting a new acquaintance. Once this information is shared, there is often an appraising eyebrow and a surreptitious look up and down to see if the demeanour and outfit match the expectations of such a role. Our worth as a human being is summed up by a job title or the company we work for.

Work values

Two key values have defined my career choice. The first is my belief in social justice for everyone. Class, colour or ability should not divide us, since we are all equal and deserving of respect. The second is advocacy and the need to provide a clear voice for the weaker or more vulnerable in society. I did not recognise these clearly in my early career, but they have guided my every action and decision. From my first days in caring roles, to Social Work and to becoming a Chief Executive for a charity supporting vulnerable adults, my need to serve others people has shined through.

When my work was closely aligned to my values I always found fulfilment in it. When I made the transition from the voluntary sector to commercial organisations it took me some time to reconnect with my core values. Although I enjoyed the challenges of the work, I missed the deeper, value-driven work of my earlier career.

I had to learn to reconnect with what was important to me, to help me make the transition to management consultancy. I started to look for projects that allowed me to support teams and coach individuals, to help them make a clearer link between their work and inner drivers. By helping to shape their connection with their values, I was able to reconnect with my own.

Being so open-hearted meant I stood out in the world of consultancy, driven as it is by the cult of ego, but I persevered. I was sometimes scoffed at, or saw career opportunities pass me by, because I was viewed as soft, but this did not detract me from my goal. Modern workplaces are crying out for a bit of heart and soul. People feel isolated, lonely and ignored in the workplace. Their plight is only highlighted when someone has the courage to stand up and show the shortcomings of the organisational culture.

Many workplaces hold a deep hostility towards their employees. Managers lead by fear, or impose restrictive working practises, which are punitive to young parents, or carers. I see time and again employers losing talented staff, for want of a little support and acknowledgement, a little bit of humanity.

I have also seen the amazing tenacity and resilience of the human spirit with people working in pressurised environments, doing exceptionally well. Some people seem to be able to rise above the chaos around them and bring out the best in themselves and everyone around them like a beacon of light and positivity.

Find happiness at work

One of the privileges I have with my line of work is being able to see into many different organisations and how people work. I have worked in multinationals, small start-ups, the public sector and the voluntary sector. From this unique viewpoint, I have observed many aspects of work and the relationships we have with our colleagues and managers.

When people feel engaged and valued at work there are no limits to what they will do. Yet when they feel disengaged and undervalued they can be resentful and unwilling to do anything to help themselves or other people around them. We all experience these contrasts at work at some point. If you looked at your situation, which one of these camps do you fall into? How do you describe your relationships at work and how do you feel about your job?

Coming Home to You

One of the traps I see many people fall into about their work and their satisfaction with it, is to assign conditions that when met will bring them happiness. They say; *"If only: my boss/colleagues would leave; I'd get promoted; I could have a pay rise..."* In the long run however, these conditions fail to satisfy. They are transitory victories, which are swept aside as soon as a new cause for unhappiness settles in. Happiness, real happiness, has little to do with external factors. It is an inner space and place, which has a constant smile and self-assuredness. Once we arrive at a place that requires no external conditions, we can find happiness in the most unlikely workplaces. As we discussed in Chapter 6: Calm the Inner Critic and Chapter 11: Find Value Beyond Money, the solution here is the same. The more we learn to love, appreciate and accept ourselves, the easier it is to accept and enjoy the place we are in right now with our work, even if the conditions are far from ideal. In his book *Happier* Tal Ben Shahar[26] encapsulates this:

> *"We cannot, though, simply hope the right job or right employer will be handed to us. We have to actively seek and create meaning and pleasure in the workplace.*

CHAPTER 12: Meaningful Work

Blaming others - our parents, our teachers, our boss, or the government - may yield sympathy, but not happiness.
The ultimate responsibility for finding the right job or creating the right conditions lies with us."

Our life purpose will be found somewhere in the simple act of giving and contributing. What we give will depend on our particular talents and gifts, but all of us come here to give and contribute to the whole. We are not single organisms, or in competition with each other to decide who gets to win. It is something that we are all gifted and capable of doing. Work is one of the places outside of the family where we can share our gift. If we arrive at our work happy, kind, considerate and compassionate, we make our day and everyone else's enjoyable; we contribute. We don't look around and feel resentful if someone else has a more favourable relationship with the boss, or compare our salaries, or workloads. We simply smile and look at how we can do the best job possible or how we can help our colleagues with their work.

Managing conflict at work

Unhappiness at work can come down to conflicts with our colleagues, such as personality clashes or a difference in working styles. Sometimes it is bullying behaviours from peers or managers. Learning to deal with these situations can mean the difference between staying in a job which you enjoy, or moving on prematurely, perhaps to less favourable conditions.

Learning to manage conflict effectively is an important life skill and nowhere gives us a better training ground than our workplace. When we are faced with a conflict, our immediate response is to personalise it and assume it is about us and how the other person views us, when in fact, the issues would have probably arisen anyway. Learning to side step conflict dynamics by not taking it personally, creates space for us to more keenly observe the dynamic that is being played out. This can be difficult when someone is being rude or aggressive, but is an important first step in getting to a resolution. Connecting with our breath will help us during these challenging times.

Conflicts and bullying behaviours are an indication of the inner turmoil and pain the other person is in.

CHAPTER 12: Meaningful Work

Rather than face their pain, they project it outwards to those people around them. This gives them relief for a short amount of time, but the pain quickly returns, leading to habitual aggressive outbursts. Once you can view the person as a victim of their own rage and confusion, it is possible to show compassion for their pain. Becoming the keen observer frees you up from your own habitual reactions and allows you to stay calm, present and sensitive.

When we reach this place of acceptance, we can work on the behaviours at hand, without losing sight of the person. A challenging colleague can be met with a smile and a soft word, whilst still holding your position and stating your needs. Simple techniques such as deep breathing into your heart and imagining a rosy glow enveloping your colleague will immediately soften the dynamics. You are literally sending love to them in an energetic form.

If the behaviour is more entrenched or it is a major transgression, address this through a more formal process. Ask for help when you need it. Never avoid these difficult conversations because the situation will rarely rectify itself without an intervention. If you have set up a meeting, ensure you are balanced in terms of your own emotions and energy to enable you to express yourself clearly. Use the questions at the end of this chapter to help clarify your thinking and express yourself objectively and unemotionally.

Managing and addressing conflict effectively is one of the best skills you can have in your toolkit. You will find your confidence grows considerably after working through issues with someone who seemed intractable. The conflict resolution muscle gets stronger with use, so never let those who are less aware of the consequences of their own behaviour spoil your enjoyment of your work.

Find your flow at work

My work brings me to a diverse range of workplaces, teams and projects. I never really know what I am going into next and no two situations are the same. I have had my fair share of unreasonable bosses, difficult teams, angry co-workers and technology spectacularly failing at a crucial moment for the business.

Some projects were challenging and I completed them with a heavy burden. Others were fun and I could not believe how quickly the time went. Regardless of the organisation's culture, I am always aware of my responsibility as a positive role model. No matter how tough the situation, I need to radiate warmth and positivity, which gives hope to other people that all will be well.

My flow, delivery and contribution is grounded in a place of purpose. I have learnt to pay attention to relationships, people and to human need first. How can I bring a smile to someone's face? How can I help make this work day easier? How can I lighten the load for those around me? The project work is delivered, but my real role is about connecting to the hearts and minds of those people around me. I can be the bridge for their change journey, opening their energy, belief and motivation to connect deeply to their own life's purpose, by showing them mine in every gesture, word and deed.

When we come from this place we are always in 'flow'; the magic place which allows us to achieve our goals effortlessly. Our energy flows like a river and we feel joyful. I see potential for learning and growth in every situation. When I am in a blaming, pressurised workplace, I look to see what I can contribute to change the culture. I do not start to identify with the way things are done. I do not start to copy the behaviours of those people around me. I observe, I smile and I look for new and gentler rituals I can bring to soften the dynamics. I give people space to express their concerns and fears and I enable them to see other ways they can react to what they are experiencing.

You can find flow by starting with your passions and interests. What is it you bring to work that is unique to you? It might be a talent with people, or with numbers, or with music, or with baking, but it is currently dormant. Look at ways you can bring this into your work life. If your talent is numbers, offer to support the accounts department, or perhaps build up meaningful reports on performance and data, which will help your team to work better. Be prepared to invest your own time to showcase your talent. Find the space and time to allow your passion and interest to shine and be seen. If it's music, but your day job is in banking, perhaps start a community choir, which can raise money for good causes and give other colleagues an outlet for their creative talents. Or if it is baking, you can start a regular coffee morning. Whatever it is you really care about, never leave it at the door when you arrive at the workplace, find a way to integrate it, to express it and allow it to do good for other people. This is the path to finding flow at work.

Mindful transitions

When you find yourself in a challenging workplace then you might need to face the inevitable decision to leave. If you cannot find a way of contributing in your current role, or the cost to your own self-confidence is too high, then perhaps you need to look for new opportunities.

The most important piece of advice I give someone who is thinking of leaving their job is, never rush. If you are in too much of a hurry to leave, you think only about what you want to get away from, and not where you are going to instead. I have seen countless times, people who leave one job in dissatisfaction only to rush to another situation that has similar issues.

Workplaces can be dysfunctional and it can be difficult to go around with a smile on your face while coping with difficult and aggressive behaviour from those people around you. There will be times when it is necessary to move on to a new workplace, but this can be achieved mindfully and from a place of inner contentment. Take your time to really think about where it is you want to go. Visualise all the aspects of the workplace and the colleagues you wish to work with, before you start sending out your CV.

The best way to find a workplace that is more in tune with your energy and your values is to attune yourself to these before you leave. The greater our alignment to the positive energy of a new working culture, the more likely the opportunity will reveal itself. When faced with hostile and difficult behaviour, if you can stay calm and polite, demonstrating the behaviours of your ideal workplace, the more likely it is the right opportunity will reveal itself. Such is the power of energy; we will always be drawn to a frequency that matches what we emit.

 **Call to action**

Work does not define us, but our thoughts around it do. We can find meaningful work through the meaning we place in it. When we are unhappy with our current circumstances, we need to look at whether the issue is an external one - the work does not ignite our passion and interest, or if it is an internal one - the work has lost its spark and flow. If we wish to find meaning in our work, we start by changing our own relationship to it. Once we can match our inner passion with our outer actions, meaning and fulfilment follow. For some people, it might mean preparing to move jobs, for others it might be a re-orientation to what is important in your current role. Exploring and testing out the issues that resonate with you will help to pinpoint the right course of action in your quest to find meaningful work.

 **Make it happen**

The first three exercises in this section are offered as standalone activities, for you to pick up and use as best fits your situation. The fourth exercise is a process taught to me by my good friend and mentor Mario Van Boeschoten many years ago, as a way of gaining deeper understanding of conflict. I have used it many times with teams I managed with great success and offer it here for your benefit. The questions and process of facilitation will usually bring some new light to the situation and make the individuals concerned less wedded to their own opinions.

1. Use a Gratitude Journal to record your experiences

    At the end of each working day make a note of the things that stand out as bringing a smile to your face. Review your journal each weekend, on a Sunday night, so you can return to work with a sense of gratitude and perspective on a Monday morning.

2. Review your happiness at work

    Take time to answer the questions, as provided below, which Tal Ben-Shahar poses in his book *Happier* about your work life.

    - Am I happy at work?
    - How can I become happier?
    - Can I leave my job and find something meaningful and pleasurable?
    - If I cannot afford to leave or, for one reason or another, do not want to leave, what can I do to make my work more enjoyable?

3. Create your Ideal Work Vision Board

    When you know you need to leave your current job, start by building a really clear image of what

CHAPTER 12: Meaningful Work

is your ideal workplace. Use a big blank sheet of paper, or a corkboard to create a vision board, building up a picture of the key components, which make up a great workplace.

- *The job itself* - the role, responsibilities, challenges, duties.
- *Your boss* - characteristics, qualities, ways of supporting you, how he/she leads you and the team.
- *Your colleagues* - how do you want people to work and interact together?
- *Working environment* - how do you want to feel in this new place? What does it need to have to make you feel able to succeed in your role?
- *Your unique contribution* - what is it that you bring which no one else can? What is different about the way you bring your gifts and talents to work which someone with similar experience and qualifications cannot? Express what it is you know, or sense, or other people have told you which makes you unique.
- *Write your CV, based on your vision board.* Once you have put richness and colour to

your vision of your new workplace. Use the language, tone, expectations and vision that matches your vision board. Start to match yourself to your ideal workplace. Make the experience as visceral as possible so you can mentally prepare to move on to your new role smoothly.

4. How to manage conflict at work

When you have an interpersonal conflict to address, use the questions below to help understand the situation.

- How were you feeling during the situation?
- What do you imagine the other person was feeling?
- What where your intentions? Or what were you trying to achieve?
- What were the other person's intentions? Or what do you think they were trying to achieve?
- What other alternatives were open to you to get a different result?
- What options were open to the other person?

CHAPTER 12: Meaningful Work

How to manage the process for more than
one person
When you are the observer of the conflict and are
able to facilitate, the following process will help.

1. Allow each person to spend time on their own or
   with an impartial helper to address the questions
   and write down their answers.

2. Bring all the people involved together to share their
   insights. Do not interrupt the person sharing their
   insights, but allow them to express their views to all
   of the questions before the other person responds
   and shares their own perspective.

3. At the end of the process, help each person to
   identify and commit to actions to support better
   working relations going forward.

"Our spirit is always looking for ways to guide us to our true nature as a loving and compassionate human being. Our job is to listen and act on these good intentions. All we need to do is open our spiritual ears and listen to the whispers of encouragement that are always coming our way."

CHAPTER 13

Free Your Spiritual Self

We have talked throughout this book about mind, body and spirit. Healthy and harmonious living requires a balance between all three elements. In this chapter, we will explore the spiritual self and what it means to become fully aware of our spiritual nature. Our spirit is the universal energy that brings life to all things and is not the domain of any one doctrine, religion or species. When we are able to connect with and explore our spiritual nature, we are naturally guided to a happier, more compassionate and enlightened life.

I have saved the most important subject to last. The one which feels like the lynch pin of our existence and yet is the most elusive. Our outer life is guided by our inner world, the place of our thoughts, feelings and beliefs. We have covered many aspects of this in previous chapters, but here we will look at the nature of our inner world. How we can come to understand it better and learn to celebrate its influence in our life.

In this chapter, we will explore:

☑ *the nature of the divine;*

☑ *the ever-expanding universe;*

☑ *the magic of the everyday; and*

☑ *how to connect to our divine nature.*

The nature of spirit – definitions

We will explore the nature of spirit, energy body, essential self and divinity in this chapter. Let me start by offering an interpretation for each, based on my own experience and exploration. None of these terms are based on, or wedded to any particular faith, religion or doctrine, yet there may be similarities between them.

- *Spirit* is the energetic force that animates all life. When we talk of spirituality, it is the awareness of this energetic force as distinct from but intrinsically connected to ourselves.
- *The Energetic Body* is the spiritual form of ourselves. It is the mirror image of our physical body in an energetic form. For our purposes, we will use energetic body and spirit interchangeably.
- *The Essential Self* relates to the point where our inner and outer life coexist. At this intersection between the two, we can blend our understanding of our present moment with the timeless wisdom present in all life.

- *Divinity* is the intentional power behind spirit to create and nourish life for the purposes of enhancement and growth.

Welcome spirit into your life

If our perspective is only what we see in our immediate vicinity, we will see trials, tribulations, war and conflict, for the world is full of it. Yet this is not the beginning, nor the end of the world. When we set our sights a little higher, reach beyond the immediate strife and ask the deeper questions, a quiet beauty emerges, of a divine universe for which we play a small but significant part.

My path to spiritual awakening was not a blinding moment of realisation, but a range of experiences, which helped me to question, explore and gain new insights. Our spiritual awakening is crucial to our transformation journey, precisely because it brings the physical and energetic sides of our nature together.

I was brought up in the Catholic faith, which like many religions has profound and loving teachings, alongside highly divisive and punitive beliefs. As a child growing up, this was deeply confusing and troubling at times and if I ever questioned aspects of these teachings or contradictions I often received a slap for being cheeky. This did little to advance my spiritual growth.

By early adulthood, I was angry with the Catholic Church and all organised religions, which I viewed as controlling, judging and exclusive. I did not relate to the image of a god, always defined as a male human figure, who seemed loving towards his own, if they met his high expectations of them and intolerant to those outside of his flock. Because I was unable to separate spirituality from religion, I rejected everything and saw myself as an atheist.

In the late 1990s I visited Thailand. It was my first experience of Asia and of a Buddhist country. I was completely overwhelmed by the beauty of the land, the gentleness of the people and the inclusivity of the Buddhist teachings. Thailand, like all modern societies has its issues, yet there is still a thread of Buddhist values visible everywhere. Buddhism focuses on our spiritual awakening as an inner journey, which deeply resonated with me. In early Christian texts, the same inner journey as the path to enlightenment is also evident, but has since evolved into different forms of church defined doctrine.

Coming Home to You

My insights from Thailand and Buddhism enabled me to understand how all religions offer an opportunity to make this spiritual connection when we come to them with an open heart and mind. Enlightenment is not the domain of the few, nor the monopoly of doctrines and religions, instead it is an inherent part of our human experience.

Many traditional texts, including: The Bible; the Qur'an; and Tao Te Ching; as well as ancient traditions such as, Gnosticism; Taoism; and indigenous cultures; talk of spirituality as separate from, but inextricably linked to the body. Despite the diversity of their geographic or cultural circumstances, they all come to view the physical existence on this earth as a product of the spiritual realm. We see a universal theme emerging, which views the spirit as the creative force that brings forth life and connect us to a greater arc of wisdom beyond space and time. They all have a version of soul or spirit, which is seen as an individual soul in the West and a great spirit in other traditions.

We do not have to wrap ourselves up in the whys and wherefores of each religion or tradition. Nor do we need to agree which one is 'The Right One', or 'The Way'. We can step back and explore more gently which one speaks 'Our Truth', which one helps us to understand our own nature. For all paths have something of value, yet no one will be universal in its application.

The miracle of life

The nature of spirit goes back to our essential nature. It focuses on the energy behind the physical body, which enables a deeper and more meaningful connection to all of life.

When we look more deeply at the world we live in and see the extraordinary gifts imbued in all forms of life to thrive, we know we live in a miraculous world. The fact we have an earth on which to thrive is nothing short of miraculous. A dictionary definition of a miracle is: *"An effect or extraordinary event in the physical world which surpasses all known human or natural powers and is ascribed to a supernatural cause."* Miracles are the events that are beyond the concepts of the human mind, but not beyond the bounds of what is possible. While our human mind is limited in perspective, imagination and ability, the universal powers that brings forth life, are not. Once we allow for the fact that miracles abound all around us, we can become relaxed and watch in wonder as the world unfolds around us.

Coming Home to You

Our planet started its journey millions of years ago, as a molten rock floating through the universe, which after a series of miraculous events, became a vibrant host of life. In his book *A Brief History in Time* Stephen Hawkins[27] captures some of the wonder of the conundrum:

"What is it that breathes fire into the equations and makes a universe for them to describe? The usual approach of science of constructing a mathematical model cannot answer the questions of why there should be a universe for the model to describe. Why does the universe go to all the bother of existing?"

While we may never truly understand the unifying force that has construed the perfect conditions to exist right here, on earth, in an ever-expanding universe, we can acknowledge its miraculous impact. When we remain enthralled to the wonder behind the mystery, we can touch a little of the magic of life and marvel at how it sustains us all.

Once we move out of ego mind, which always places us at the centre of the universe and we move to a place of wonder and gratitude of what is, we start to live a wonderful and enraptured life. We are inspired by the miracle of life that abounds all around us. The self-sufficiency of all species to adapt to its habitat, to draw what it needs to survive and flourish. Once we stop working out the *'Who'* behind all of life and accept the *'What'* of its existence, we can start to put our faith in a much greater force that is behind all of life.

Oneness

Every living organism on this planet and indeed in the universe is powered by the same energy source, which many ancient wisdoms describe as oneness. Separation between humans and between all life forms they tell us is only an illusion. Thich Nhat Hanh[28] a renowned Vietnamese Zen master captures this:

"Insight is our liberation. Insight liberates us from our fear, our ignorance, our loneliness and despair. It is this insight that helps us to penetrate deeply into the nature of no-birth and no-death, and the interconnected nature of all things."

The concept of oneness can be very difficult for the Western mind to understand and accept. Driven as our society is by egocentric living, we view individuality as the ultimate state of achievement. Our physical body becomes our focus and this blinds us to our spiritual nature and our connection to all that is. The body is only an extension of the spirit and the spirit has an unbroken link to all of life. Spirit has no form and all forms. It is in every aspect of the earth's energy, in all life forms and in every star and planet in the universe. Since we all come from the same unifying source of energy, we are all one.

Embracing the concept of oneness can bring enormous comfort. Leaning into oneness, is allowing life to simply be. When we no longer see ourselves as separate from each other, where are the grounds for conflict? When we no longer see ourselves as separate from the earth and the other species on it, where is our motivation for destruction? Oneness may be a difficult concept to fully embrace yet it can bring a profound shift in our mindset when we can open ourselves to the implications of what it can teach us. This is the path to true enlightenment; our ability to see the light in the world in all its forms.

Become less egocentric

In earlier chapters, we looked at the ego mind and its important function in our survival, but also its destructive nature when it takes over our lives. It is difficult to get the balance between our ego and our essential self and in some spiritual and personal development circles the ego becomes demonised. True enlightenment we are told will only come if we kill the ego. This is rather drastic and misses the point of our human existence. The ego is part of our evolutionary journey. It is the safety mechanism that enables us to cope with an uncertain world and is part of the reason we have evolved to become the most successful species on this planet. The ego is a storehouse of all our memories and all our experiences. It makes linkages between current and past events, which in times of danger can make the difference between life or death. Its strength is also its limitation, since the ego is concerned with past and future, it will constantly shift between these two points in its keenness to work out what is happening and whether the current situation poses any danger. This continually distracts us from the present moment, which is the only place where we can experience oneness.

Coming Home to You

The ego is not our enemy, but neither is it a true friend. The ego is like an inconsiderate guest we welcomed into our home and before we know it, has claimed a stake in every room and started to dictate terms of how we live. It will start to control and dominate every aspect of our lives unless we learn to recognise it, tame it and ultimately create distance between it and our true self.

Taming the ego is rather like house training a puppy; it takes time, patience, repetition and loving compassion. Our ego is still an important aspect of our life, acting as it does as an early alarm system for danger, or a reminder for us to not repeat a past mistake. We want the ego to function at what it does best and keep doing it. Beyond this, we need to control the ego's influence on what we think and feel. In areas such as relationships, our work and mental health, we are better served by the essential self, which sits behind the ego. Where the ego has muscled in and made us arrogant, obsessive, anxious or emotionally remote, we need to recognise and mitigate its influence through more mindful living.

In Chapter 6: Calm the Inner Critic, we discussed the insistent voice in our mind and finding a place of inner calm. It is often the simplest techniques, practised regularly, which can have a big impact in reigning back our ego. Some of these techniques are described at the end of this chapter, including: Gratitude Journals; Mirror Work; Silence; and Personal Mantras.

Rise to a higher plane

Changing our thoughts is a way of altering the frequency of our energy. As in the experiments with the rice described in Chapter 6, the impact of our thoughts on ourselves and environment are profound. When we choose combative and destructive thoughts they create negative energy and when we choose gentle thoughts they create positive energy. Our route to the higher plane of consciousness is through the quality of our thoughts.

To increase our energy vibration and move to a higher frequency, we need to learn to simply be. When we are in the present moment, accepting everything around us, exactly as it is, without narrative, judgement or an inner call for action, we become calm and light. We create the space to transmute our energy from a heaviness that literally weights us down, into a joyous inner peace that naturally uplifts us.

Being in the present moment requires us to let go of our egocentric lens, which compares, contrasts and categorises what we see in the world, which in itself creates separation. We can minimise the impact of the judging lens of our own thoughts and those of other people by staying anchored in the present moment. It does not mean we no longer listen, simply that we do not accept wholeheartedly the views presented to us, preferring instead to stay open, connected to the present moment and maintaining our inner peacefulness.

Anchoring our thoughts in a deep contemplative observation of the present moment gives us focus, perspective and allows us to see the whole rather than fragmented pieces.

Our energy naturally changes to a higher, lighter frequency when we become more contemplative. We see the physiological changes as well because we learn to relax our muscles, feel a loosening of our chest and allow our breath to deeply fill our body and soul. When we move into Being rather than Doing, we become a radiant, peaceful and happier version of ourselves. This is the key to our journey to a harmonious life and it takes one important step to make it happen: surrender.

Surrender to the source

The term surrender has negative connotations to our modern mind, associated as it is with winning or losing. If I win, you lose and vice versa. One of us must surrender to bring victory to the other. Seeing surrender in these binary terms, makes it difficult for us to welcome it into our hearts.

Another way surrender can be interpreted, is giving up the ego mind as the centre of our orbit. When we accept there is a much bigger force at play around us, one which surpasses beyond measure what our ego mind can construe, then surrender brings with it freedom. To express gratitude and wonder for the greater wisdom at play in all of life and feeling comfortable allowing it to guide our actions is a form of surrender. After all, if the universe can conspire all the miraculous events that created a stable planet for us to survive and thrive on, then it's not too big a leap to suppose there is a nurturing force behind us, willing us to succeed.

Surrendering to such a force allows a much deeper wisdom to emerge. This form of surrender has nothing to do with ego; it transcends it. We surrender to the bigger tapestry of life, trusting it will always sustain and support us, as it always has. In the beauty of surrender, our eyes are opened to the magic around us. The famous poet, William Blake[29] captured this magic.

"To see a World in a Grain of Sand
And Heaven in a Wild Flower,
Hold Infinity in the palm of your
hand And Eternity in an hour."

By embracing and celebrating the greater mystery of life that abounds all around us, rather than analysing, compartmentalising and labelling it, we can be filled with the same sense of wonder.

Learning to surrender takes patience, since we have built up a lifetime of striving, controlling, planning and struggling. These patterns do not disappear overnight and will take effort to resist their familiar call of 'Doing'. Doing is sexy. Doing is active. Doing is strong. Doing is our way to avoid difficult and painful emotions. Being, on the other hand, is still. Being is silent. Being is observant. It is the most difficult state for us to remain in, driven as we are by motion. Oriah[30], in her book *The Call* describes this constant pull between the two states:

"Every time I let my actions be distracted solely or primarily by the desire to create change, no matter how lofty or spiritual the cause, I am rejecting what is and so causing suffering in myself and the world."

The irony of our situation is we must learn to come to a place of complete stillness to allow us to move to a place of meaningful action. As Oriah said, *"If we move from a place of desire, it will be our ego mind which wants to fix things."* When we come from a place of Being, we know there is nothing to be fixed, for everything is perfect as it is. Once we have this deep inner acceptance of the world, our being can guide us to contribute and enhance what already is. When we act from a place of Being, it is focused and considered, deeply connected as it is, to our intent and the needs of the world. It does not have strife or suffering within it, since love is the driving force.

When we allow the light and power of love to guide our thoughts, feeling and actions, it has an incomparable quality to when we are pushing, controlling and doing. In the last chapter, we looked at how to find our flow and this occurs when we come from a state of Being. We align ourselves to a greater universal power, which will bring harmony into every moment of our life. The nature of Being is described in the *Tao Te Ching*[31], a 3,000-year-old text from China. The words are enigmatic and at times contradictory, but always profound. The ancient text says of Being"

"In Tao the only motion is returning. The only useful quality, weakness. For though all creatures under heaven are the products of Being. Being itself is the product of Not-being."

We are reminded in this last phrase, of the eternal energy that has brought us to life and will continue to exist when our human body has perished. Non-being is the on-going consciousness found in the universe. The invariable constant which will go on with or without us. All life returns to the source; the only motion is returning. When we accept this certainty, we truly free our spirit to live the most rewarding and happy life possible.

 Call to action

Our spiritual nature is not to be viewed as a distant cousin who we only see occasionally, or a pious aunt who drives us to be fearful of the wrath of an almighty being. Our spiritual being is a part of our everyday lives. It is in the smile we give to a passing stranger, or the generosity we show a person in need, or in the gentle manner we display to a young child. Our spirit is always looking for ways to guide us to our true nature as a loving and compassionate human being. Our job is to listen and act on these good intentions. We do not need to strive, push, or punish to bring out a better side of ourselves, for it is there, waiting to show up in the quiet moments of our lives. All we need to do is open our spiritual ears and listen to the whispers of encouragement that are always coming our way.

 Make it happen

1. Keep a gratitude journal

    At the end of every day write down 10 things you are grateful for. It can be profound things such as the love of your partner, or simple things such as the bus being on time for work. Using a Gratitude Journal helps us to appreciate the many areas of our life, which bring us happiness.

2. Mirror work

    Every morning, before you leave for work, look at yourself in the mirror and smile. Say to yourself, *"I am a confident, capable and compassionate person. Today will be a good day, because life loves me."* Look into your eyes as you repeat the phrase five times. Notice your breathing and emotions as you repeat the phrase. Do this exercise for a week and journal any changes you notice.

3. Practice silence

Practicing silence consciously can bring us closer to our inner life. Commit to an hour when you can be alone, free of interruptions and practice being silent. If outside, be aware of any tendency to greet others with a word and instead use a smile and nod of the head. If inside, cut distractions such as music, televisions and mobile devices. Let yourself relax into the silence and just notice the world around you without narrative. Journal your insights at the end of your session.

4. Develop a personal mantra

Louise Hay in her book *You can Heal your Life* was a great proponent of using mantras to change our thinking. What mantras create is a space in our mind for new ideas to break through the barrage of repetitive patterns from the ego. A few simple words repeated silently, during times of transition, change or anxiety will help to restore peace of mind. Here are a few examples: *"All is well"; "I am open to love"; "Life loves me"; "I choose happiness."* For more mantras to help you in a variety of situations visit my website: www. findyourjoyfullife.com.

Harmony
Change
Courage
Timeless
Joy
Intent
Meaning
Wholeness
Compassion
Energy
Belief
Peace
Love

"Taking the journey home to you, one step at a time will reap the most amazing rewards. Be free, be brave and enjoy every minute of this wonderful life you have."

Learn to Come Home to You

If you have come to the end of the book, you may have a lot of questions and thoughts in your mind about how to put these ideas into action. You may also have a lot of doubts about how and where you can start to practice these new concepts and whether you will feel defeated, overwhelmed or both, before you have even had a chance to begin.

Firstly, relax. All of these doubts, concerns and fears are perfectly natural when you come face to face with the challenges of change.

Secondly, I reiterate what motivated me to write this book in the first place, which was my belief that we all have potential in us to achieve great things. We are capable of living a fulfilled, happy and healthy life, despite the many messages to the contrary that swarm all around us. If you have come to the end of this book, you will know my journey transformed from one of happenstance, struggle and illness, to living the most joyous and enlightened life imaginable. I do not think I am unique and I truly believe the same is possible for you.

If you are struggling to know where to start, here are two simple steps you can take right now:

- reduce the amount of time you spend reading and listening to the news and media; and
- become more mindful of the images you portray on social media and less willing to complain or gossip about other people.

We become more balanced in ourselves when we do not allow our energy to be expended on the everyday dramas that play out around us. Instead, look for positive outlets for your energy, where your kindness and compassion can shine through.

At the end of this book is a section on recommended further reading. It is consciously small, to not overwhelm you, but do not feel limited by the suggested texts or the ones mentioned in the reference section. It is a big world out there, with many books that might equally help you along your journey. Be bold and explore.

If you have a specific area of your life where you need further help and signposting, here are a few suggestions.

Become braver about making change and decisions in your life

The hardest part of making a change is overcoming the initial fear about whether you are capable of making it, or whether it will bring the anticipated results. We are all in fact, built-in change machines, but fears and anxieties have become endemic to our modern way of living, stifling our abilities. If this feels like a particular challenge for you, Chapter 2: The Nature of Change and Chapter 4: The Power of Intent, will help you to find a new way of framing change. The two things, which help us overcome the fear of change, are a clear vision of what we want to change and creating life enhancing habits to help us achieve it. The exercises at the end of these chapters will help you do this. On my website: www.findyourjoyfullife.com, you will find an Interactive Exercise to help you build your own vision board, which can be a powerful tool to galvanise your efforts and propel you forward.

Move from a life of struggle to one of abundance

It can often feel hard to see abundance in your life, when all you see around you is struggle and hardship. If you are worrying about how to pay your utility bills or cover your rent or mortgage payments, life does not feel abundant at all. Even from a place of relative financial security, you might still find yourself worrying incessantly about whether you will ever have enough money to feel secure. Chapter 11: Find Value Beyond Money, provides insights and practical tips on how to rebalance your relationship with money. Chapter 8: Timeless Living will also help, since abundance is as much about our relationship with time as it is about material goods. Learning to turn our relationship with time around to one of free-flowing engagement will bring us closer to abundant living. If after rereading the chapters and doing the exercises you still have further needs, sign up to one of my Abundant Living webinars, where we explore the subject in more detail in small groups with interactive discussions.

Awaken your sense of self and connect to your inner world

If you feel this is where you are on your journey, you may have found that Chapter 5: The Nature of Consciousness, Chapter 6: Calm the Inner Critic, on controlling your thoughts and Chapter 13: Free your Spiritual Self, to be the most useful. If you still have some questions about where and how to start, reread these chapters and make the time to do the exercises at the end. Particularly, I encourage you to concentrate on forms of meditation, which can bring the quiet moments of inner discovery you may be looking for.

In addition, you will find powerful guided meditations on my www.findyoujoyfullife.com, each with a specific goal or issue in mind. I also recommend reading Eckhart Tolle's book *The Power of Now,* which provides great insight in how to live joyfully in the present moment.

Personal transformation and spiritual awakening

If this book has made you hungry to learn more about personal transformation, there are lists of further reading materials in the next section and on my website. If you are curious and willing to learn, you will find that all sorts of books and experiences turn up to help you. See my suggestions as a starting point rather than a definitive list. You may also benefit from more interactive events such as workshops or webinars. Look out for events posted on **www.findyourjoyfullife.com**, but also look to other centres for personal development, which can offer events with a mixture of learning, reflection and group discussion.

Your first next steps

If you are still unsure about where to start, I urge you to start somewhere. There is an old saying, which speaks a good truth: *"How do you eat an elephant? One bite at a time!"* The same is true for your own journey of change. As tempting as it might be to try everything all at once, this is likely to overwhelm you and ultimately lead to failure. Be kind to yourself and choose one area of your life, or one new technique you wish to master and do this for the next three weeks. Use a journal to record and notice the changes, since the memory can be a fickle thing. If you see benefits, continue with what you are doing. If you feel resistance or difficulty, move on to another technique or focus on another area of your life.

The point is to keep moving, to keep experimenting and experiencing and most importantly to enjoy the journey and learn along the way. After all, isn't this the very essence of life? Taking the journey home to you, one step at a time will reap the most amazing rewards. Be free, be brave and enjoy every minute of this wonderful life you have.

If you want to contact me, please do so using any of the following.

Email: mary@findyourjoyfullife.com

Website: www.findyourjoyfullife.com

Twitter: @marytmcguire

Further Reading

The Surrender Experiment by Michael A Singer

This is one of the best books I have read about how to understand and tame the ego. It is easy to read and full of insights about how our thoughts work and the benefits of freeing ourselves from them.

The Power of Now by Eckhart Tolle

This is a classic text in the self-help arsenal, yet when Eckhart Tolle had his flash of insight, he was homeless and living on the streets. He describes why living in the present moment is the only moment we have and what the consequences to us and our world are when we fail to do so.

The Call: Discovering Why You Are Here by Oriah Mountain Dreamer

This is a seeringly honest account of striving to achieve a spiritual life, only to realise it is the striving

that is getting in the way. Oriah shares her journey and realisations in this short and easy read.

The Tapping Solution: A Revolutionary System for Stress-Free Living by Nick Ortner

If you are in physical pain or struggling with stress, anxiety or overcoming a difficult past, this book will help. Nick has taken a well know technique and made it very accessible. He also has many freely available resources on his website: www.nickortner.com

A 1,000 Words for Joy by Byron Katie

This book reads like a stream of consciousness from Byron Katie, where every page literally jumps with joy. At the heart of the book is her technique 'The Work', which involves applying four seemingly simple, but in fact, very searching questions to areas of our life where we are struggling or have conflict. It will give you tools to practice, as well as an encouraging journey to give you hope in yours.

References

Chapter One: My Story

1. **Einstein, Albert**, Quote "The Definition of insanity is doing the same thing over and over again and expecting a different result." Attributed to Albert Einstein from his letters of 1920 – 1936, but has equally being attributed to Benjamin Franklin, Mark Twain and others.

2. **Dyer, Wayne**, Quote: "We are Spiritual beings having a temporal experience in a physical body." The source of this quote is much disputed. Wayne in his work attributed it to Jesuit Mystic Pierre Tielhard du Chardin, an influential spiritual teacher of early 20th century France . I have left it attributed to Wayne Dyer, since he was the most recent proponent of the idea, but the concept can be found in all ancient wisdom traditions including Buddhism, Hinduism, Christian Gnosticism and many native and tribal communities such as the Native American Indians.

Chapter Two: Embrace Change

3. **Kubler-Ross (1969)** *Death and Dying*. In the book she proposed a five stage model of grief. This was later adopted for business and popularised by Fisher John, (1999) Originally presented at the Tenth International Personal Construct Congress, Berlin, 1999, and subsequently developed in his work on constructivist theory in relation to service provision organisations at Leicester University, England

4. **Frankly, Viktor (1992)** *Man's Search for Meaning*. Quote: "In a position of utter desolation, when man cannot express himself in positive action..."p.39. he described this on his long walk to the first labour camp, when he was sure that his parents, his wife and her parents had by now perished. He expresses his wish to stay connected to some inner drive of acceptance to help him go on with life, when everything felt so worthless.

CHAPTER 3: Control Your Emotions, Control Your Life

5. **Loyd, Alexander and Johnson, Ben (2011)** *The Healing Code*. The technique is described in Chapter 10 of the book.

6. **Ortner, Nick (2013)** *The Tapping Solution*. The book builds on the work of Gary Craig from the EFT Manual, which in turn builds on the ancient arts of energy medicine from China. Ortner's version is accessible and easy to read and has become very popular as a result.

Chapter 4: The Power of Intent

7. **Jordan, Michael**, US Basketball Player, widely believe to be the greatest of all time. As a motivational speaker, he talks about failure as part of life. Failure is not the issue, it is giving up, or not trying harder that is the issue. His quote "I've missed over 9,000 shots in my career. I've lost almost 300 games. 26 times..." was first published in Nike Culture: The Sign of the Swoosh (1998), by Robert Goldman and Stephen Papson, p. 49, but has widely quoted ever since as a great example of why failure and success go hand in hand. The failure to achieve something brings important lessons that when applied brings rewards.

8. **Hill, Napoleon** (2009) *Think and Grow Rich*. The quote about "What the mind can conceive and believe, it can achieve" was attributed to the qualities of these extraordinary industry magnates who had become successful, despite the odds against them. The book talks about the quality of our thoughts creating the quality of our reality. For Hill three qualities were essential to success: Desire, Faith and Perseverance. All success starts in the mind.

Chapter 5: The Nature of Consciousness

9. **Penrose, Roger (1989)** *The Emperor's New Mind* "I would say the universe has a purpose" Penrose has written many books on the connection between fundamental physics and human (or animal) consciousness. In The Emperor's New Mind (1989), he argues that known laws of physics are inadequate to explain the phenomenon of consciousness.

10. **Bruce Lipton**, a pioneer in the field of genetic research and consciousness, called epigenetics, said: "A person's health isn't generally a reflection of genes, but how their environment is influencing it..." His work can be found at: https://www.brucelipton.com/resource/article/epigenetics

Chapter 6: Taming the Inner Critic

11. **Byron Katie with Stephen Mitchell** (2008) *A Thousand words for Joy*. The essence of Byron's work is to question every thought we have and test whether it has any fact in it. In her process 'The Work' the main question that is asked is 'Is this thought true? How Do I know it is true?'. More details can be found at: http://thework.com/en

12. **Emoto, Masuru** (2005) *The True Power of Water*. Emoto was a Japanese researcher who started to experiment with the quality of water by exposing it to different environments.

Chapter 7: As Without, so Within

13. **The World Wide Fund for Nature** (WWF) *Living Planet 2016*, which showed the startling loss of life between 1970 and 2012. The loss of life in vertebrates is startling, but even more so in freshwater species such as amphibians which are down 81 per cent. The full report can be downloaded at: http://www.worldwildlife.org/pages/living-planet-report-2016

14. **The World Bank** collects data from over 140 countries from subjects as wide as Gross Domestic Product (GDP) and Population. They have one of the most reliable databases on human growth available. Further details can be found at: http://datatopics.worldbank.org/hnp/popestimates

15. **The Food and Agriculture Organization (FAO)** of the United Nations published the report predicting a human population rise of over 30 per cent and the need for food production to increase by over 70 per cent. See: http://www.fao.org/fileadmin/templates/wsfs/docs/expert_paper/How_to_Feed_the_World_in_2050.pdf. The FAO is an agency of the United Nations that leads international efforts to defeat hunger.

16. **Compassion in World Farming** (2012) *Food Sense*. The report highlights the huge waste in modern farm practices resulting in farm animals competing with humans for the same food. See more here: https://www.ciwf.org.uk/media/5161445//foodsense.pdf

17. **Advocacy for Animals** (2015) *Dairy Farming* In their report from Lorraine Murray, they look at dairy production. See here: http://advocacy.britannica.com/blog/advocacy/2015/05/dairy-farming-still-big-business-big-trouble-for-cows/ Advocacy for Animals campaign and raise awareness of the plight of farm animals, mainly in the USA.

18. **Our World in Data**, report large increases in life expectancy since World War 11. See: https://ourworldindata.org/life-expectancy/

Chapter 8: Timeless Living

19. **Tolle, Eckhard** (2011) *The Power of Now*. This book was written based on his experiences, including a time living on the streets. He realised that inner calm and peace was available to him wherever he was, if he took time and pleasure to enjoy the present moment, the only moment that ever really exists. The quote comes from Chapter 3: Moving Deeply into the Now, which is all about living timelessly.

Chapter 9: Coming Home To You

20. **Singer, Michael** (2016) *The surrender Experiment*. Singer has also written another fine book called 'The Untethered Soul'. Both talk about spiritual awakening, but it is in this his first book that his personal journey emerges from an Economics graduate to a multi-millionaire corporate executive, before retiring to writing and mindfulness teaching. After his moment of clarity in 1971, he allows his life to unfold according to what is placed in front of him, rather than anything that his own ego mind would push him to do. What unfolds is the most extraordinary journey, rich with experience and contribution to millions of lives.

21. **Saha, Mille** (2011) *The Twelve Principles of Light*. Dr Saha shares her wisdom openly in this book which explains the principles of healing, the energy body and the importance of the energy centres, known as chakras.

Chapter 10 Courageous Living

22. **Galloway, Steven** (2008) *The Cellist of Sarajevo*. A work of fiction, which reimagines the siege of Sarajevo from the perspective of four protagonists. Interestingly the Cellist is not one of them, but becomes a sign of hope and is to be kept alive by the sharp shooting female sniper Arrow. A wonderful novel about how humanity can emerge even in the most inhumane places.

CHAPTER 11: Find Value Beyond Money

23. **Institute for Fiscal Studies** (2016) *The Gender Wage Gap*. This white paper highlighted the gender pay gap across all sectors and found that men got paid on average 20 per cent more than women and in some sectors the gap was considerably larger. Full report available for download at: https://www.ifs.org.uk/uploads/publications/bns/bn186.pdf.

24. **Franklin, Benjamin** "Money has never made man happy, nor will it, there is nothing in its nature to produce happiness. The more of it one has the more one wants." The actual source of this quote is hard to find, so this may be attributed to the great man, rather than his own words.

CHAPTER 12: Meaningful Work

25. **Chartered Instituted of Personnel and Development** [CIPD] (2016), *Employee Outlook, (November)* Quarterly outlook report found that satisfaction at work continues to be very low.

26. **Shahar, Tal Ben** (2008) *Can you learn to be Happier?*, P99. The quote is from Chapter 7, Happiness in the Workplace. Shahar talks about the difference between *Hard* currency of money, that we work for and the *Ultimate* currency of our happiness, which has a deeper choice attached to it.

CHAPTER 13: Free Your Spiritual Self

27. **Hawkins, Steven** (1995) *A Brief History of Time*, P. 192 *"What is it that breathes fire into the equations and makes a universe for them to describe?"* Perhaps the most famous quote of a highly quotable book on life, our planet and the birth of the universe. Hawkins does not describe himself as religious in the traditional sense, but shares his awe of the universe and its wonders.

28. **Thich Nhat Hanh (2014)** a renowned Vietnamese Zen master has written many books on Buddhism and the concept of Oneness. This quote was taken from a blog post: 'The Moment is Perfect, June 16, 2014. You can access the full article at: https:// www.facebook.com/notes/mystic-sounds/the-moment- is-perfect-by-thich-nhat-hanh-/535779769861985/

29. **Blake, William** (1801) *Auguries of Innocence*. The famous quote "To see the world in a grain of sand..." comes from this poem. He was not widely recognised during his lifetime, but afterwards his works were given great merit, as luminary and prophetic.

30. **Oriah** (2005) *The Call*: *Discovering Why You Are Here. "Every time I let my actions be dictated by..." p.12.* Her book is a very honest account of her own struggle with doing and recognising that only by being, could she discover her own Call.

31. **Tao Te Ching by Lao Tzu** (300bc) [Author], translated by Arthur Waley (1999). There are many translations of this enigmatic text, but Arthur Waley's is seen as authoritative